All the World's a Stage

All the World's a Stage

Developing and Implementing an Inclusive Theatre-Based Faith Community

DEBORAH L. RICHARDSON-MOYLAN

Foreword by Robert K. Johnston

WIPF & STOCK · Eugene, Oregon

ALL THE WORLD'S A STAGE
Developing and Implementing an Inclusive Theatre-Based Faith
Community

Wipf & Stock
An Imprint of Wipf and Stock Publishers
199 W. 8th Ave., Suite 3
Eugene, OR 97401

www.wipfandstock.com

PAPERBACK ISBN: 979-8-3852-5696-9
HARDCOVER ISBN: 979-8-3852-5697-6
EBOOK ISBN: 979-8-3852-5698-3

01/23/26

To Tom, Leighton, Cameron, and Libby, the loves of my life

Contents

Foreword

IN HER OPENING SOLILOQUY in the movie *Bull Durham,* groupie Annie Savoy explains why she loves the "church of baseball." She confesses that she previously gave Jesus a chance but it didn't work out because "the Lord laid too much guilt on me . . . You see, there's no guilt in baseball and it's never boring."[1] As a young Christian in junior high going to a lively large church with a great youth group, my friends had the same reaction whenever I would invite them to our church. They would come once and then either make some excuse for not coming again, or flat out say to me it was boring and too heavy. The gospel for them was not heard as "good news," regardless of the intention of our youth leaders or my own experience.

Here also is the context for Deborah Richardson-Moylan's book *All the World's a Stage: Developing and Implementing an Inclusive Theatre-Based Faith Community.* Given her Pentecostal church on the one hand that feels an obligation to defend "truth," and given the theatre community in most cities including hers that feels committed to creativity and new expressions of beauty, "being boring and laying on too much guilt" is an altogether predictable response to the church by those in her town's theatre community.

Of course, all such tensions have only been radically heightened by the differences between many evangelical churches and the wider community when it comes to issues surrounding LGBTQ+ persons. The rejection by many evangelical churches of LGBTQ+

---

1. Shelton, dir., *Bull Durham.*

activity and the wider artistic community's overwhelming acceptance of diverse sexualities has created an almost unbridgeable chasm. In such a context, Deborah asks, how can the gospel actually be received today as "good news"? It is the right question! And her book gives readers one practical answer through her outreach to her local theatre community. Here might not be the "answer" to all aspects of this cultural divide, but in a context in which we as a culture and we as a church need desperately to move beyond stark polarities, it is a wonderful model generated by love.

Given the increased polarization of American society in all areas, but also, and perhaps particularly, with reference to sexuality, where people are encouraged to hold on to one of two extremes without nuance or qualification, middle-ground solutions are of yet few and far between. Here is the strength of Deborah's response.

FAITHFULLY ORTHODOX AND/OR RADICALLY LOVING

Experiencing the culture's widespread change in their understanding regarding sexuality, the church has found itself hard pressed to know how to be understood as loving unconditionally while continuing to teach a traditional biblical understanding of sexuality. While Elton John might not be the most impartial observer, his caricature of the church, like most caricatures, unfortunately contains too much truth to be ignored:

> Religion promotes hatred and spite against gays . . . But there are so many people I know who are gay and love their religion. From my point of view, I would ban religion completely. Organized religion doesn't seem to work. It turns people into really hateful lemmings and it's not really compassionate.[2]

It has seemed too often that the evangelical church must choose between being perceived as "faithfully orthodox" or being perceived as "radically loving." The American culture has largely

2. John, "Interview."

accepted the LGBTQ+ community as part of our beautiful rainbow of humanity. Even by 2010 movies and television shows had multiple hits with relatable, everyday gay/lesbian characters—*Modern Family*, *Glee*, *The Good Wife*, *Ugly Betty*. By 2015, thirty-six states approved of the marriage of same-sex couples and almost three-quarters of the American population today agree.

With such changes in our culture's understanding of sexuality, the church has found itself struggling. While fifty years ago, many church members had little to no experience with LGBTQ+ people, that is not the case today. With the growing cultural acceptance, churches find increasingly that many of their members have family or friends that are openly part of the LGBTQ+ community. UCC and Episcopal denominations were the first to use "a canon within the canon" to say that whatever being faithful biblically might mean, love must be at the heart of the Christian response. But today, all Christian communities are being pressed to show how they are in fact "loving." When asked in 2013 about a purportedly gay priest, even Pope Francis said, "Who am I to judge?" And in 2023, the pope allowed priests to bless (though not perform the marriage of) same-sex couples. The times, they are a changin'.

Within the evangelical church in America, support for gay marriages has been growing, though acceptance is by no means the norm for most evangelicals at an institutional level. According to one poll, for example, support for gay marriage among younger evangelical individuals increased between 2003 and 2014 from 20 percent to 42 percent. And most observers today believe that a majority of younger evangelicals support gay marriage. Certainly in my congregation that is the case. Similarly, an increasing number of pastors, though by no means the majority, are now in favor of the full acceptance of LGBTQ+ people in their congregations, including supporting their lifelong marriages. Perhaps as telling, two of evangelical's leading scholars writing on human sexuality, David Gushee and Richard Hays, have reversed their theological positions on sexuality, now fully accepting gay marriages. Gushee's book, *Changing Our Mind*, came out in 2017. Hays's book, *The Widening of God's Mercy* (2024, written with his son Christopher

Hays), was perhaps even more important, for this New Testament scholar's treatment of a biblical understanding of homosexuality in his *The Moral Vision of the New Testament* (1996) had been the most frequently used text by evangelicals for twenty-five years to buttress their position that homosexual activity was biblically forbidden.

Evangelical churches find themselves struggling theologically given those in their church with gay family members, given America's almost univocal acceptance of a gay lifestyle in entertainment and politics, given those under forty who have grown up in a culture that has empowered gays/lesbians and considers this normal, given leading scholars both within and beyond the evangelical church who are questioning or have rejected traditional biblical interpretations as unbiblical, and given society's rejection of evangelicals' plea that they really are "loving people" despite their theology of rejection. In this situation, books like *All the World's a Stage* are increasingly important if the evangelical church's witness to the gospel, the "good news" of Jesus, is any longer to be heard by others in America.

TWO QUIET EXAMPLES

At the 2025 Emmy Awards, perhaps the most surprising trophy that was given went to Jeff Hiller for "supporting actor in a comedy series." Hiller was not on anyone's list to win. His small show on HBO, *Somebody Somewhere*, largely flew under the radar. However, voters recognized Hiller's portrayal as singularly important. Mary McNamara, critic for the *Los Angeles Times* wrote:

> Playing Joel, a gay, devoutly Christian man in a small town, Hiller fearlessly leaned into dichotomy and sincerity, which is very difficult to do . . . There was nothing flashy or predictable about Hiller's performance. A deceptively quiet role in a deceptively quiet series. It was astonishingly powerful.[3]

---

3. McNamara, "Night's Best and Worst Moments."

Fearlessly leaning into dichotomy and sincerity, Richardson-Moylan has also crafted her own deceptively quiet response to how the evangelical church might engage the theatre community in her small town. Nothing flashy, but astonishingly powerful. The gospel is being heard as the "good news" that it is.

ROBERT K. JOHNSTON
Senior Professor of Theology and Culture
Fuller Theological Seminary
Pasadena, California
September, 2025

Preface

THE JOURNEY HAS ENDED, but has also just begun. My journey of creating a new church expression for theatre artists in North Central Massachusetts, one that is also welcoming and inclusive of LGBTQ+[1] people, has concluded. The church gathers consistently every month and will for the foreseeable future. There is much for readers to learn about the process I observed to create this faith family in the pages that follow: context, procedures, experiences, and constructive critical reflection. What is not included in this project are my continuing experiences that inform and strengthen the why of my doing so as well as those that feed my passion to continue.

I have recently directed a play entitled *right before i go* (lack of capitals by design from the playwright), written by Stan Zimmerman. The play deals with the difficult topic of suicide and uses Zimmerman's experiences as a gay man who lost his gay best friend to suicide as the foundation for the piece. It then weaves together both his story and the suicide notes of others that have died by suicide. Many of those whose letters are quoted are from the LGBTQ+ community. In addition, the cast included a trans woman whose first public theatrical performance as a woman was this very play.

After opening night, an audience member who knows that I am also an Assemblies of God (AG) pastor came up to talk with

---

1. I have used the term LGBTQ+ throughout my original writing, but have honored other terms as published in works that are cited.

me on his way out. With tears in his eyes, he said, "As a gay male who grew up in the AG, the fact that you present these plays is incredibly healing." After our second evening performance, a cast member told me that her lesbian friend, also raised in the AG, asked her, "What's up with your pastor?" She then said that this friend wanted to meet with me to discuss this juxtaposition of my leadership in an AG church and my role as theatre producer who uses theatre to bring justice to the oppressed, including the LGBTQ+ community.

These two individuals represent the hundreds, if not thousands, of LGBTQ+ people that have left evangelical churches due to their sexual orientation or gender dysphoria. They did not want to leave Jesus, but they had to leave the church because the environment was toxic to them.

My own fellowship, the Assemblies of God, is a Pentecostal conservative fellowship of churches that has consistently held to the belief that homosexuality is a sin. Their position paper on *Homosexuality, Marriage, and Sexual Identity* states:

> It should be noted at the outset that there is absolutely no affirmation of homosexual activity, same-sex marriage, or changes in sexual identity found anywhere in Scripture. Male and female genders are carefully defined and unconfused. The consistent ideal for sexual experience in the Bible is chastity for those outside a monogamous heterosexual marriage and fidelity for those inside such a marriage. There is also abundant evidence that homosexual behavior, along with illicit heterosexual behavior, is immoral and comes under the judgment of God.[2]

Conservative theology does not allow for an alternate reading of Scripture. However, as an ordained minister in the Assemblies of God, I am not required to affirm the position papers. My renewal each year requires that I have preached the gospel for the past twelve months, that I have given my tithe, and that I affirm the *Sixteen Fundamental Truths*.[3] I sign my renewal each year, and

2. AG.org, "Homosexuality, Marriage, and Sexual Identity."
3. AG.org, "Assemblies of God Sixteen Fundamental Truths."

sleep well, knowing that I have done just that. Even so, I know that those that I love and care for in the LGBTQ+ community are aware of the AG's stance on homosexuality, and hence their confusion with the seeming contradiction of my pastoral leadership and my role as theatre artist.

I hold these two lives in tension, knowing that at any time I may have my credentials questioned by those that are in leadership within my fellowship. After having posted something on social media that identified me as an ally to the LGBTQ+ community, I received an email from a pastor in my region. He questioned why I would post such a thing, what it meant, and if I had a doctrinal change. I called him immediately to have a conversation. During our discussion, I was given multiple stories of those that he knew that he said had "left the gay lifestyle." Although I respect him and his ministry, I was disappointed to hear him use this phrase. It indicates a belief that one can just set aside an integral part of who they are. I then countered that I knew just as many or more stories of those that had been wounded by people that claim to represent Christ in more conservative churches. Specifically, I shared a story of someone that grew up gay in the AG and was encouraged to be diligent in prayer in order to change his homosexuality. He went on to attend an AG college, was married, had a child, and then could not keep up the façade any longer. Not only did the more conservative stance damage this individual, it also negatively impacted his wife and child.

I then decided that I needed to talk with someone in my fellowship about this book and the possible ramifications of it. I called someone that I respect within the Assemblies of God and asked to meet in person. We discussed the email from my associate, the content of this book, and a podcast that I had produced. I was encouraged to persevere until the energy required to deal with my detractors became detrimental to following the call of God on my life as I see it and know it.

It is possible that those in my fellowship will believe I have gone too far, and those on the more liberal theological spectrum that will believe I have not gone far enough. Living in the tension of both these worlds has helped to craft my book and has also allowed me to have a platform from which I can minister to those from the LGBTQ+ community that have left the Assemblies of God as well as other conservative denominations. It is my prayer that healing will happen and a shift will be made, for the sake of the gospel and the lives that could be impacted by it.

Acknowledgments

I AM SURROUNDED BY those that continually encourage and challenge me to become the best version of myself possible—thank you for praying and believing.

First, I would like to thank the community at Fuller Theological Seminary and Dr. Robert K. Johnston for providing the means for me to explore, engage, and grow.

Thank you to the editorial and production staff at Wipf & Stock, who not only saw the potential of this book, but created a process in which to bring it to fruition.

I am grateful to the beautiful people of Sanctuary Ministry Center, who have made serving in ministry a joy in so many ways. They have allowed for my quirkiness as a lead pastor and have loved me through all the ups and downs of planting a new church. I have seen the miraculous in their midst and have been so blessed to be their pastor.

I will forever be grateful to those that decided to try something new and who began to travel a journey of discovery as theatre artists and seekers of community and truth within *Dinner Theatre . . . Church?* Even though our logo included a question mark after "Church," we have discovered together that we are definitively a church in the most beautiful of ways.

I also want to thank those that have created art with me through the avenue of City on a Hill Arts. I could not do it without the dedicated artists that have called this production company home, especially David, Bethany, Sarah, and Jack. Thank you for catching the vision and helping bring it to life. May these stories continue to impact and change our communities, fostering a more just and loving response.

I am grateful to all my friends and family that are part of the LGBTQ+ community. Thank you for trusting me with your stories, and for allowing me to share my life with you.

I want to honor my mom, Sheila, as the first person to show me that education is a lifelong pursuit. She was my role model in attempting advanced degrees no matter our age. May this book honor her memory.

For my children, Leighton, Cameron, and Libby: my role as mom to you three is my greatest joy. You astound me every day and I hope that you will continue to impact the world with your gifts, talents, and hearts. You truly are gifts from God for which I am deeply, deeply grateful.

For my husband and best friend, Tom, who did not know he married a future pastor when we first said "I do"—thank you for allowing me to thrive, for encouraging me, and for being my sounding board. You complete me.

And finally, I am so grateful for Jesus—savior, redeemer, friend—my life is changed forever.

Introduction

My INITIAL GOAL WHEN beginning this journey was to reach unchurched people that are part of the theatre community in North Central Massachusetts. The means to do so was to develop a new inclusive church expression comprised of theatre artists and to implement a means of constructing dialogue in the *lingua franca* of the theatre for the purpose of discipleship in matters of faith.

THE STATE OF THE CHURCH

Massachusetts was founded by the Puritans—a separatist group seeking to create the epitome of a religious community. John Winthrop had hoped to create a "city on a hill" (referencing Jesus' words as recorded in Matthew 5:14). Jonathan Edwards preached his sermon *Sinners in the Hands of an Angry God,* in Northampton, a town in western Massachusetts. Adoniram Judson and others were the first American missionaries sent overseas, sailing from Salem, Massachusetts to India. Massachusetts has a proud history as the birthplace of Christianity in the United States and the birthplace of overseas missions. Today there is little that resembles the fierce religious fervor that marked Massachusetts in its first two centuries.

National Church Trends

In general, church attendance in the United States is steadily declining. As reported in *The Guardian,* "Protestant pastors reported that typical church attendance is only 85 percent of pre-pandemic levels . . . while research by the Survey Center on American Life and the University of Chicago found that in spring 2022, 67 percent of Americans reported attending church at least once a year, compared with 75 percent before the pandemic."[1] It is even more dramatic when it comes to emerging generations. In addition, *The Guardian* reports, "But while Covid-19 may have accelerated the decline, there is a broader, long-running trend of people moving away from religion. In 2017 Lifeway surveyed young adults aged between eighteen and twenty-two who had attended church regularly, for at least a year during high school. The firm found that seven out of ten had stopped attending church regularly."[2] This reporting confirms the general decline of church attendance along with the steep decline within emerging generations.

Massachusetts Church Trends

My particular context is New England, specifically Massachusetts, but much of what I learned demographically can certainly be extrapolated for other locations. Massachusetts statewide has seen a radical change in church attendance. There are other areas of the country where churches abound and church attendance is culturally prevalent, but not in Massachusetts. According to the Pew Research Center, Massachusetts has the following reported findings:[3]

- Only 58 percent of adults consider themselves Christian, of which only 9 percent are evangelical. The majority of those that consider themselves Christian are Catholic.

- Thirty-two percent of respondents are classified as "unaffiliated" or "nones."

- Only 40 percent of Massachusetts adults are certain in their belief in the existence of God.

1. Gabbatt, "Losing Their Religion," para. 7.
2. Gabbatt, "Losing Their Religion," para. 8.
3. Pew Research Center, "Religious Landscape Study."

- Only 33 percent of adults consider church attendance important, while 20 percent don't think it's important at all.

- The majority of adults in Massachusetts don't attend religious services at all. Only 23 percent attend once a week (a 7 percent decline in seven years), while 40 percent seldom if ever attend a worship gathering (a 12 percent increase in seven years).

- Religious education or discipleship has taken the hardest hit, with 75 percent of adults stating that they seldom if ever attend any deeper learning.

- Fifty-four percent of adults no longer believe that the Bible is the word of God.

The data all point toward a decline in church attendance, a decline in the belief in God, and a denial of the authority of Scripture. One area that still holds strong is hope: hope in something more. Most adults in Massachusetts still hope in the truth of heaven. An ember remains of Massachusetts's former spiritual fervor.

CHURCH PLANTING AS A POSSIBLE ANSWER

One of the ways to fan that remaining ember into a flame is church planting. C. Peter Wagner has been credited with stating that the single most effective evangelistic methodology under heaven is planting new churches.[4] While that may be true in some states, and in some countries, it is not necessarily true in Massachusetts. I have served on the Missions Committee of the Southern New England Network of the Assemblies of God. We recently did a survey of church plants since 2000. Of 107 churches planted in the past twenty years, forty-one have closed. Many more are barely surviving, having not developed past dependency on a parent church or the Southern New England Network itself.

4. Wagner, *Church Planting for a Greater Harvest*, 11.

Fresh Expressions of New Church Plants

Church planting as a method of church growth and multiplication has begun to see a metamorphosis into what is called fresh expression churches. These can include dinner churches, hiker churches, forest churches, and more. According to Steve Pike, "The 21st century culture is rapidly diversifying and churches that thrive in the 21st century will reflect that diversity."[5] The basic premise is that these unique expressions of church will attract and serve smaller demographics that would not typically enter a traditional church building. Instead of planning a large and splashy church launch with facilities all in place and a full staff, these gatherings are defined by their intimacy and shared experiences.

An Expression Just for Theatre Artists

The premise of this book—a faith community for theatre artists—takes root in the soil of the fresh expression movement. I am not a typical pastor—even though I am not certain of how that would be defined. There are times when I wonder what I am doing and if this is what I am supposed to do with my life. Then there are times when I can fully embrace my call and I feel as though I am operating directly in the center of God's will. What makes me an atypical pastor is that I am a woman, an actor, and a musician. In addition, I am an LGBTQ+-affirming ally ordained in an evangelical fellowship. Often, I feel like a square peg in a round hole.

I planted a new church in 2013 in the hopes of reaching the theatre and creative community in North Central Massachusetts. My heart has always been to create a safe place for people that do not normally fit into society. The theatre community is one such demographic. They are self-defined outsiders, of which I am one. My husband has consistently told me that the theatre community is my church. When the church I planted did not develop into what I had hoped, I was disappointed. The truth is that other unchurched people arrived—other people that had been ostracized or wounded

5. Pike, *Next Wave*, ch. 10.

by people within Christ's church. They, too, were welcomed into our midst because we had created a safe place. I yearned to create a safe place for theatre artists to gather and discuss topics of faith, all the while celebrating their creative uniqueness.

Why Plant a New Church?

Although many might wonder if planting a new church is necessary given the number of existent churches in any given city or town, a church designated for a unique demographic could be necessary. One of my goals was to discern if creating a faith family out of the theatre community was even possible. If the religious temperature of Massachusetts has decidedly cooled over the past two centuries, it is downright chilly and brisk when it comes to theatre people and their relationship with the historical Christian church.

THEATRE COMMUNITY AND THE CHURCH

I took an informal poll of Central Massachusetts theatre artists to gauge their affinity toward or against Christianity. Out of seventy-nine respondents, the results reveal:

- 26 percent—I am positively inclined toward Christianity and participate regularly in events.

- 11 percent—I am ambivalent toward Christianity and only participate in major holidays when convenient.

- 26 percent—I am negatively inclined toward Christianity and am not one to participate in any way.

- 20 percent—None of these options describe me.

Added by respondents:

- 16 percent—I am positively inclined toward Christianity and negatively inclined toward its use to discriminate against others, participating selectively.

- 1 percent—I am negatively inclined toward Christianity but participate on holidays for the non-religious meaning behind them (e.g., being with family).

This is quantifiable feedback, but my own experience within the theatre community here in North Central Massachusetts, while not quantifiable, is just as valid. I moved to my current hometown in 2000 and have invested more than twenty years of my life into the theatre community. I am an actor, director, music director, and producer, having been involved in scores of productions over the years. By being personally invested, I have been able to develop trust and I love the people in my theatre community. Through countless conversations over the years, I have learned of the deep wounds that affected so many in the theatre community by people in the church. I have also learned of their true desire to explore the deeper things of faith, coupled with the reticence to ever walk into a church building.

THE PREMISE OF THIS BOOK

It is the premise of this book that there is a place where theatre and church intersect, that by creating a unique space and setting, theatre people will find a place of welcome as well as a safe place in which to discuss faith, or the lack thereof, without judgment and without fear. It is also the premise of this book that to create that space, a new form of church has to be developed. This new form must be outside the constructs of traditional church structure. Language has to be adapted so that the language of the Christian faith and the *lingua franca* of the theatre community is woven together in such a way that the discussions do not seem foreign, but rather, familiar and comfortable. Finally, it is a premise of this book that there is a way to bridge the gap between Pentecostal theology and queer theology in such a way that the life-changing power of the gospel can work in tandem with the radical love of Jesus so that members of the LGBTQ+ theatre community can experience that radical love through a life-changing encounter with Jesus without condemnation or rejection.

THE LAUNCH OF DINNER THEATRE . . . CHURCH?

To begin the journey of creating this community, I launched a fresh expression of the church specifically geared toward theatre people. According to Lifeway Research, an important quality of new church plants includes relationship development rather than a launch model. "The focus of the church planter often becomes less about how to gather as many people as quickly as possible, to how to be a gospel witness that is meaningfully engaged and making disciples within a hard-to-reach community."[6] I was engaged within the theatre community for more than twenty years, so it was time to convert that relational currency into an intentional community. Over the course of one year, I hosted informal gatherings under the title of *Dinner Theatre . . . Church?* Invitations were made, mostly over social media, to the wider theatre community in North Central Massachusetts. Each week the number of attendees grew until eventually twelve consistent theatre artists came together to form a group. This group met for over a year and shared meals, conversations, and the support of the community. The challenge was to discern how to disciple this group in matters of faith, with the goal of leading people into an understanding of the basic precepts of the Christian faith. It is through these dialogues and much research that I was able to develop a collection of theatrical and theological writings that would eventually be used to bring this new faith community closer to an understanding of the basic teachings of Jesus: love, grace, mercy, and more.

During this season, I lived a double life: leading a traditional Assemblies of God church on Sundays, while gathering with this unique and beautiful group of theatre people on Wednesday nights. The juxtaposition of both was messy, but it was rewarding and wondrous.

6. Yang, "Four Trends Shaping Church Planting," para. 23.

BOOK OUTLINE

In part one of the book (this Introduction and chapter 1), I lay the foundation for the need for a new expression of church within this theatre demographic. An essential aspect of part one is relationship-building with those in the theatre community and interviews that will establish everyone's experience with the Christian faith, revealing areas that might still need resolution or healing.

In part two (chapters 2 and 3) I lay the theological groundwork for a theatre church along with spiritual development that is affirming, loving, and healing. I begin by dialoguing with other literary works to draw comparisons between theatre and church in the areas of God's presence, embodied discipleship, and enacted justice. I also establish the theological foundations for developing new expressions of church within, and for, the theatre community. Finally, in part two I address the seeming contradictions between Pentecostal theology and queer theology to establish a safe space to encounter the truth of the gospel for LGBTQ+ individuals.

I include in part three (chapters 4 and 5) the research that is the foundation for the faith family as well as the means to develop this community. I follow the journey of developing a theatre faith community as well as the coordination and implementation of a collection of various works of writing geared toward the discipleship of that faith community. I outline in part three a twelve-month journey culminating with a celebration and reflection on what was accomplished over those twelve months.

Conclusion

A year of launching and experiencing *Dinner Theatre . . . Church?* has revealed the need for this community. A series of podcast interviews that I recorded after the one-year anniversary will share the impact of this gathering for those that are members.

Chapter 1

The Foundation
of a New Church Expression

I AM AN ASSEMBLIES of God pastor, ordained in 2014. Yet, my history with God's church is varied and mixed: I was raised in a Presbyterian church, but I walked away in the 1980s and explored New Age and Wiccan communities. I returned to the Christian faith in 1992 and began to attend a United Church of Christ church, went to seminary, and transitioned to the Assemblies of God. My journey has been one of multiple expressions of church, which has served me well.

THE FIRST STEP: SANCTUARY

In 2010, I began to feel the stirring to plant a new work. At that time, I had been serving as a worship arts pastor in an Assemblies of God church. I had hoped to plant this new church with the blessing of my senior pastor, but unfortunately that was not to be. After much heartache and emotional abuse, I left my church and spent a year healing, all the while sharing the vision of a new type of church, where people from all walks of life could come together and feel safe. This was the beginning of what is now Sanctuary

Ministry Center, a new church that was planted in a small, rural town in Massachusetts, officially launching in September 2013.

Traditional Was Not The Intent

Although Sanctuary was birthed out of the desire to reach a community that was unreached by traditional church models, the form and function of church planting into which I was thrown helped create a very traditional church in many ways. The metrics that determined success helped to create a boilerplate-style church. These metrics included: women's and men's ministries, a worship leader, a kids' ministry leader, a certain quantity of adherents, and more. These metrics were tied into funding that helped to secure my adherence to these expectations. I also did not realize there was any other way to create a faith community. Even with these constraints, I began to cast vision and mission that aligned with my heart for those that were far from God or wounded by their experiences with Christ's church.

Some of the foundational core values that we began with in 2013 include:

- Sanctuary is a safe place where one can explore their faith without judgment, and where we encourage others to become all that God has created them to be.

- Sanctuary is a safe place for families to become strengthened and secure; where children are free to be kids while they explore their own faith journeys.

- Sanctuary is a safe place to explore one's creative side. We believe that the arts are an expression of the creative Spirit in each of us and are a valued expression of our faith.

Much of what I had hoped would develop included a place for artists to come to faith. What happened was that other people, not necessarily artists or creatives, came into our midst seeking that safe place. It became evident to me during that season that there are many who have had negative experiences within organized religion, and many have been wounded by church people. Yet, they still want to believe in a God that loves them. They have a heart to learn more and draw near to God. Sanctuary became that place, and remains that place for many, but it became abundantly clear that I needed to do something else to minister to the artistic community.

Theatre Outreach to Children

To begin to reach creatives I first started a theatre camp during the summer for kids in our community. This summer camp was an alternate experience to the traditional Vacation Bible School. These theatre camps were faith-based, but included theatre, dance, and music training, with a performance at the end of the week. We filled our school's gym with kids that loved to perform, and showed the love of God while they were with us. I also ran an after-school theatre workshop program for the elementary kids within our town. Although I was able to make wonderful connections with the children, the goal of reaching creatives in my community for Christ was not being met.

City on a Hill as an Outreach to Theatre Artists

The next step was to create an arts ministry arm of Sanctuary, which I entitled City on a Hill Arts. For the first few years of its existence, City on a Hill Arts was an extension of Sanctuary. We began by presenting a dance production, then moved on to producing other theatrical pieces. Our first year we produced one work, and then grew to produce two per year. In many ways I felt overwhelmed by the work of it: the church by and large did not support the theatrical endeavor, therefore much of the work to produce these pieces fell on me and a small group of people. In addition, I was still unable to make any real impact on reaching creatives for Christ.

CITY ON A HILL MOVES OUTSIDE THE CHURCH

When the COVID pandemic hit, I decided that City on a Hill Arts needed to be its own entity. I created a separate 501(c)3, asking some dear friends to sit on the board—friends that were not necessarily Christian. This was in direct response to some counsel that I had received: the board of any organization must reflect the people that the organization wishes to serve. If I wanted to reach the LGBTQ+ community, I had to ask someone from that community to sit on the board. I would never have been able to do that if City on a Hill Arts had remained under the auspices of Sanctuary, so separating the two was the right decision.

The board of City on a Hill Arts began to refine the values and mission of City on a Hill, reflecting God's heart for justice. Right out of the pandemic we produced *The Crucible, The Diary of Anne Frank,* and *The Laramie Project.* The goal was (and continues to be) to produce works that fostered dialogue surrounding the juxtaposition of faith and culture, and how our faith might inform our choices. We hoped to foster a more just and loving response in our audiences after having experienced our productions. We included talk-back evenings so that the audience could engage with the artistic team and the cast, thereby creating even more opportunity for dialogue.

It was through City on a Hill Arts that I began to see that a theatre faith community might still be possible, just not in the form of a traditional church. If the productions and the impact on our audiences had been enough, I could have stopped there. Although I was developing a strong community of performers and artists through City on a Hill Arts, the intentional discipleship and dialogue that could occur through a faith community was not happening. The people with which I was coming into contact knew what I did for my day job or, as I referred to it with them, my consistent Sunday morning gig. They would ask sporadic faith-based questions in response to things happening within our community or the world. Occasionally, someone would approach me for prayer, but that was the extent of my theological or spiritual impact.

THE SPIRITUAL TEMPERATURE OF THEATRE
ARTISTS

All the questions and requests for prayer revealed a group of people that were curious, even positively inclined toward knowledge of Jesus, but had no place where they felt comfortable satisfying their curiosity or learning more. A very small percentage of the North Central Massachusetts theatre community are churchgoing people. Conversely, many have walked away from their childhood faith due to trauma or lack of acceptance. I began to wonder if there was a place where these individuals could go to ask questions, be loved for who they were, and feel safe doing so.

The theatre community is oftentimes neutral to the church. Not everyone that is part of the theatre community is against the church, but it has been my experience that most theatre artists in North Central Massachusetts are, at best, neutral toward the Christian faith, if not downright negative. This is not surprising given the general makeup of theatre artists: self-defined outsiders that have found community within theatre itself. Historically, evangelical churches have created boundaries between who is in and who is out. Typically, artists and creatives have been deemed out for centuries. Couple that with the high percentage of the LGBTQ+ community that have found a home within the theatre community and it is understandable that the church has been viewed as unaccepting and unwelcoming, maybe even hostile. I agree with Makoto Fujimura that we need to create cultural contexts where a love toward those outside our tribe's borders is cultivated and organically modeled.[1]

In addition to these concerns is the culture and dynamic of theatre itself. Community is something that develops during the production of a show: friendships are made, emotions are intense, and memories are created. When the show closes, most of the people involved go back to their lives, never connecting on that level again until the next show. Nothing exists to bridge the gap between shows, leaving people generally without community. Presenting a

---

1. Fujimura, *Culture Care*, 66.

possible bridge to community was and is part of the goal of this new church expression.

THE LGBTQ+ COMMUNITY AND JESUS

During the early part of the COVID pandemic, I was involved in a production of *Legends and Bridge*, a comedy in which I played the role of Judy Garland. The cast consisted of five people: three women and two men. Also involved in this production, which was rehearsed for a live-stream performance, included the director and the stage manager. Of the cast and crew, only two members identified as straight (heterosexual). The balance of the cast and crew identified as bisexual or gay. Two men were engaged to be married to each other, and one man had been married to his husband for more than thirty years. The youngest gay male cast member grew up in the Assemblies of God.

We had rich conversations about Jesus, faith, and the church during our rehearsals. The truth is, those conversations were some of the most in-depth I had experienced in a long while, and they did not occur in a traditional church. These people loved Jesus but did not have a place where they could worship or where their love of Jesus could be fostered and their sexuality affirmed. They knew I loved them and they trusted me to share their experiences and concerns.

CONCLUSION

The few months I worked in a COVID-pandemic production were eye-opening in many ways. It became apparent that a different form of church was in order: one that would gather the theatre community with the intention of developing community and dialogue. I took Jesus as my role model, he who had spent countless hours around tables, pouring into people both life and love. Fujimura states it beautifully: "It is time for followers of Christ to let Christ be the noun in our lives, to let our whole being ooze out like a painter's colors with the splendor and the mystery of Christ, the inexhaustible beauty that draws people in. It's time to follow the Spirit into the margins and outside the doors of the church."[2] It was time for me to get outside the walls of traditional church and offer something new to these people that I love. The gathering of this community and the development of a new expression of church with theatre artists as the core group is the purpose and result of this book.

2. Fujimura, *Culture Care*, 85.

Chapter 2

General Revelation
and Embodied Discipleship

Much of theatre involves experience, narrative, and embodiment. Therefore, if one desires to create a faith community developed from the theatre community, it must include those same three elements.

In this section I dialogue with a variety of authors that are able to address the gamut of these three elements. The authors address experiencing the Divine outside of traditional church, the narrative of Scripture and how we fit into it, and learning through various systems of embodiment.

GENERAL REVELATION AND HOLY THEATRE

In this section I deal with experiencing the Divine in, and through, theatre. Therefore, I have chosen Peter Brook's influential work *The Empty Space*, because he draws many parallels between theatre and church, exploring sacred forms and rituals. To counter Brook's secular voice, I include and dialog with Robert Johnston's *God's Wider Presence* and Kerry Dearborn's *Drinking from the Wells of New Creation*. These authors make solid defenses for

God's presence outside of what is knowable through the Bible or the church, in addition to focusing on God's revelation through the arts.

In Brook's seminal work *The Empty Space* he devotes an entire chapter to the concept of Holy Theatre. He begins by stating, "I am calling it Holy Theatre for short, but it could be called The Theatre of the Invisible-Made-Visible: the notion that the stage is a place where the invisible can appear has a deep hold on our thoughts."[1] He goes on to say that "many audiences all over the world will answer positively from their own experience that they have seen the face of the invisible through an experience on the stage that transcended their experience in life."[2] The premise of this book includes the idea that God's presence can be experienced outside of the four walls of the church, and can be experienced in a community of theatre artists on a journey toward God. In *God's Wider Presence*, Johnston affirms Brook's postulation by suggesting that general revelation recognizes that God reveals Godself not only through Scripture and in the believing community but also through creation, conscience, and culture.[3] Theatre is one aspect of culture in which God's presence can be made known.

The Celts were a people that lived according to an understanding that God's presence was available to them daily through all aspects of their lives. According to Dearborn in *Drinking from the Wells of New Creation*, for Celtic Christians all parts of life were seen in sacramental ways, as God's gracious offering and as signs of God's redeeming presence. Because of this awareness the arts were honored as a means of experiencing Christ.[4] Johnston agrees by quoting Solzhenitsyn, "Art can warm even a chilled and sunless soul to an exalted spiritual experience."[5] Johnston and Dearborn highlight an important point: the arts are a unique opportunity to experience God's presence and should not be relegated to the

1. Brook, *Empty Space*, 42.
2. Brook, *Empty Space*, 42.
3. Johnston, *God's Wider Presence*, 9.
4. Dearborn, *Drinking from the Wells of New Creation*, 128.
5. Johnston, *God's Wider Presence*, 33.

margins. Rather, the arts are a means of hearing from God as well as communicating to God. Dearborn draws the parallel with speaking in tongues: "This is the power of the arts—it is the modern-day 'tongues' in which people can hear God speaking to them in ways that they can understand, which goes beyond language barriers."[6] It is more than a one-way conversation that flows from God to people. In the same way as tongues are a way for the Spirit to speak when we don't have the words, the arts are a way for individuals to communicate to God when words are not enough.

Although Brook wrote in the late 1960s and was fairly pessimistic about the status of the theatre at the time, there is much that speaks to the juxtaposition of theatre and the church today. It is possible that we can hear the voice of God through Brook's writings—that his words were prophetic for us today in both theatre and church. For example, Brook proposes that if the need for a true contact with a sacred invisibility through the theatre still exists, then all possible vehicles must be re-examined.[7] The vehicle of *Dinner Theatre . . . Church?* that I created is one such vehicle that must be examined. It is not what Brook was directly referring to, but the combination of theatre and church is just the vehicle to meet a need for contact with a Sacred Invisibility, even to the present day.

Brook takes some time to develop the connection between theatre and church when writing about an experimental theatre group led by Jerzy Grotowski in Poland:

> Here there is a similar relation between actor and audience to the one between priest and worshipper. It is obvious that not every one is called to priesthood and no traditional religion expects this of all men. There are laymen—who have necessary roles in life—and those who take on other burdens, for the laymen's sake. The priest performs the ritual for himself and on behalf of others. Grotowski's actors offer their performance as a ceremony for those who wish to assist: the actor invokes, lays bare

6. Dearborn, *Drinking from the Wells of New Creation,* 145.
7. Brook, *Empty Space,* 48.

what lies in every man—and what daily life covers up.
The theatre is holy because its purpose is holy; it has a
clearly defined place in community and it responds to a
need the churches can no longer fill.[8]

Again, Peter Brook was prophetic as to the state of the church today. It is necessary to examine the way in which the body of Christ is creating space, or not, to allow God's presence to be made known outside of the Sunday morning gathering. The creation of art, and specifically theatre, is one of many vehicles to offer, in a ritualistic sense, a means to experience God's presence. Creating art is an act of faith, offered in faith. As Johnston writes, "While there will always be mystery that surrounds us on all sides, and though we can never know fully about that which lies behind what we create, that is exactly the point. Why there is painting, or poetry, or music at all is precisely because through them we are at times ushered into the Presence of something 'More.'"[9] His list is incomplete as it does not suggest the beauty of theatre as a means of ushering people into the presence of something more. Theatre artists have the potential to act as priests, leading people to experience the holy through their art.

Brook continues to draw the image of artist as prophet in our time:

There are two ways of speaking about the human condition: there is the process of inspiration—by which all the positive elements of life can be revealed, and there is the process of honest vision—by which the artist bears witness to whatever it is that he has seen. The first process depends on revelation; it can't be brought about by holy wishes. The second one depends on honesty, and it mustn't be clouded over by holy wishes.[10]

The artist bears witness—testifies—to the Invisible, whether or not the artist would affirm a belief in Christ or attend the local church.

8. Brook, *Empty Space*, 60.

9. Johnston, *God's Wider Presence*, 198.

10. Brook, *Empty Space*, 58.

As Johnston writes, "God's people do not have a monopoly on his revelation."[11] Each revelation, each experience of the Divine, the Transcendent, or the Invisible, is unique to each person and cannot be duplicated or manipulated. Johnston concludes that "rather than being the possible experience of every person, at all times, everywhere, God's wider revelatory Presence is instead the specific experience of people sometimes and on some occasions."[12] All we can do is faithfully curate those moments in which someone, somewhere, could possibly experience God's transforming and redeeming presence, whether that is through community or through performance.

Encountering God through the Performative Arts— General Revelation in Practice

One of the first questions I asked the fledgling community of theatre artists was: "How have you experienced the Divine or experienced a transcendent moment in theatre?" The responses that I received are covered in greater detail as I bring this book to a close, but for now it is imperative to know that the arts, and specifically the performative arts, are a means by which many theatre artists experience the presence of God or something akin to a transcendent, Divine encounter. I specifically focus on theatre in this book, but aligned with theatre are other performative arts, including television and movies whereby people encounter God. Therefore, in this section I juxtapose *Watching TV Religiously*, by Kutter Callaway and Dean Batali, with *Deep Focus*, by Robert K. Johnston, Craig Detweiler, and Kutter Callaway. From these two books we can gain an understanding of reverse exegesis and how to read culture to discern God's presence.

In *Watching TV Religiously*, Callaway and Batali attempt to show how watching TV goes beyond the explicitly religious into the implicit theology embedded in television programs, as well as

11. Johnston, *God's Wider Presence*, 98.

12. Johnston, *God's Wider Presence*, 189.

the spirituality embedded in those programs.[13] This is important to my premise because of the direct correlation between the explicitly religious in theatre pieces as well as the implicit that exists if we mine for it. This mining allows for a greater depth of theatre pieces that can speak about issues of faith without having to use explicitly religious material. In *Deep Focus*, Johnston, Detweiler, and Callaway state simply that "movies are more than entertaining diversions from what matters; they are life stories that both interpret us and are interpreted by us."[14] For the theatre community, live performances are those same powerful stories that both interpret, and are interpreted by, the audience. Johnston, Detweiler, and Callaway go on to say that "as our institutions have lost their cultural cachet, stories have emerged as our primary medium for making meaning. Our hunger for story corresponds to our growing transcendence gap."[15] Many of the theatre artists within this new community expressed an experience of the Divine or Transcendent in pieces that were not outwardly religious in content, but the stories were able to open them to that experience.

Television and movies are much more pervasive in American culture and have a greater impact on culture than theatre for most Americans. Yet, for the theatre community, theatrical live performative pieces are on an equal footing with the more popular prerecorded performative media. According to Callaway and Batali, "Television is culture creating. And it is this culture—one mediated by television—that the community of faith is called not only to understand but also to engage with wisdom, wit, and clarity. In other words, a thoughtful engagement with TV is as much about mission as it is about meaning."[16] If one agrees with this premise then the next step is to draw an extension to theatre as well. For the theatre community, it is imperative to experience, produce, and create those pieces that actively engage with the culture and current events. Johnston, Detweiler, and Callaway speak to this

13. Callaway and Batali, *Watching TV Religiously*, 6.

14. Johnston et al., *Deep Focus*, 17.

15. Johnston et al., *Deep Focus*, 64.

16. Callaway and Batali, *Watching TV Religiously*, 11.

response to culture by highlighting some of the movements in our culture such as civil, women's, and LGBTQ+ rights, that have advanced the voices of the underrepresented in film. They also ask a pertinent question: "Were film critics and theologians responding to cultural shifts or initiating them?"[17] Although theatre does not necessarily have as powerful of an influence on the larger culture as television or film, culture influences theatre. Those involved in the theatre community in North Central Massachusetts, and specifically City on a Hill Arts, are striving to produce works that give voice to the underrepresented in theatre. It is through the agency of theatre that the City on a Hill Arts producers believe they can influence the culture around them.

As stated previously, Callaway and Batali believe that engagement with TV is as much about mission as it as about meaning.[18] In the same way, engagement with theatre is as much about mission as it is about meaning. To reach the theatre community, one must be engaged with what is being created so that interaction with the theatre artists is well-informed and not ignorant of those topics of import to the theatre community. If one is on mission to the theatre community, or to any community, it is imperative to be immersed in their culture.

Callaway and Batali introduce the idea of how to analyze TV in a community of interpreters. They include a few things to assess, including how to discover or construct meaning from one's encounter with a TV program, how to examine why it worked for them in an affective or aesthetic level, and then to discuss this assessment with a broad community of TV viewers and creators.[19] This translates well into the theatre community, especially a community of faith made up of theatre artists like the one that is the subject of this book. To draw meaning from one's experience of theatre, one needs an assessment guide such as the one that Callaway and Batali suggest. For example, if one were to sit through *Les Misérables* within the context of community, the first

17. Johnston et al., *Deep Focus*, 105.
18. Callaway and Batali, *Watching TV Religiously*, 11.
19. Callaway and Batali, *Watching TV Religiously*, 40.

assessment would most likely reveal a myriad of answers as to how the community experienced the piece either affectively or aesthetically. Constructing meaning would also fall into an assortment of categories as well, depending on each person's background and experiences. The greatest value would be the discussion of these two topics within the safety of community, especially if placed in the context of a possible revelation of God's presence as experienced through *Les Misérables* itself. As Johnston, Detweiler, and Callaway write, "If viewers will join in community with the film's storyteller, letting the movie's images speak with their full integrity, they might be surprised to discover that they are hearing God as well. If we allow ourselves to be open to others, the Other might also prove to be present."[20] We can engage with the Creator through a creative medium, engage its elements in community, and possibly hear the still small voice of God through the process.

Dealing with performative art in the context of theology requires a reverse exegesis—reading culture and finding God within it, rather than imputing theological constructs onto theatre, or television. Callaway and Batali address the many ways that Christians have engaged with television.[21] These are important, because they represent the many ways that Christians have engaged with theatre as well. They include avoidance, caution, dialogue, appropriation, and divine encounter. Our goal as missional Christ-followers is to move others from avoidance to divine encounter. In addressing the history of the film rating system, Johnston, Detweiler, and Callaway posit, if theologians and church-related film critics were to have any voice at all in this new situation, they would need a broader and more informed approach to a Christian understanding and interpretation of film than the traditional rhetoric of caution or even abstinence. Dialogue, not censorship, was being called for.[22] As they stated, somewhere between avoidance and divine encounter is dialogue. According to Callaway and Batali, "Unless we are willing to open ourselves up to our

20. Johnston et al., *Deep Focus*, 149.

21. Callaway and Batali, *Watching TV Religiously*, 112.

22. Johnston et al., *Deep Focus*, 33.

conversation partners—to take the risk of being affected, informed, and enriched by them—it is difficult for any real conversations to take place."[23] One of the greatest challenges of my wearing two hats (one pastoral, one theatre producer) is encouraging my more conservative parishioners to experience things that might challenge their worldview. According to Johnston, Detweiler, and Callaway, Christians embody a wide spectrum of responses to film, and by default, theatre: preaching avoidance, expressing caution, entering into dialogue, appropriating insight, or being surprised by God's presence.[24] My more conservative parishioners, and those of like mind, continue to exist on the avoidance end of the spectrum. Yet, the only way to grow, to understand others in our community, is to engage with those topics that might seem uncomfortable.

The goal, then, would be moving people toward a divine encounter. A theatre piece does not have to be *Jesus Christ Superstar* or *Godspell* for someone to experience the Divine as audience or actor. In the same way, one does not need to watch *Touched by an Angel* or *Saving Grace* on television to experience the Divine. Yet, what these types of pieces allow is the beginning of dialogue that could quite possibly lead to that divine encounter. According to Callaway and Batali, "What these explicitly transcendent shows primarily offer is a starting point for talking about the divine more so than an actual experience of the divine."[25] This is important because it allows a bridge from one point on the trajectory to the next. This is applicable for both believers who struggle with engaging performative art, and those that do not yet affirm faith in Christ, because they can experience the art for art's sake without necessarily affirming the content. Dialogue is still possible, no matter where they might land on the axis.

Finally, Callaway and Batali propose the idea of curating our television watching fodder from the glut of digital material available.[26] This is something that I will address later in this chapter, but

---

23. Callaway and Batali, *Watching TV Religiously*, 124.

24. Johnston et al., *Deep Focus*, 114.

25. Callaway and Batali, *Watching TV Religiously*, 132.

26. Callaway and Batali, *Watching TV Religiously*, 183.

for now, it is important to draw that same parallel to our theatre experiences. With what is being produced for the stage, it is possible to curate a collection of theatre pieces that can inform who we are and how we experience the Divine. In order to develop a collection of art pieces, whether they are film, TV, or theatre, that allow us to experience the Divine in a deeper way, Johnston, Detweiler, and Callaway suggest that the thousand-year-old practice of *Lectio Divina*,[27] as well as medieval biblical interpretation, could help chart a way forward for theological interpretation of film.[28] In addition to film, it is possible to approach theatre pieces within the same fourfold construct: literal interpretation, allegorical interpretation, tropological interpretation, and anagogical interpretation.[29] Taking my example from *Les Misérables* earlier, we might experience it in the following ways, using this fourfold methodology: literal interpretation (bishop gives candlesticks to Valjean); allegorical interpretation (like Valjean, we experience mercy in a powerful way); tropological interpretation (as we accept mercy from others we then extend it as well); and anagogical interpretation (as Valjean receives mercy from the Bishop, we are offered mercy and grace through Jesus Christ). This is a relative simplification of the storyline, but if we are to use theatre missionally, a deeper look into these pieces is required.

EMBODIED DISCIPLESHIP: ENACTING JUSTICE

The process of discipleship is one of the challenges when creating a fresh expression of church that does not fall into a preconceived mold. In this final section I engage four works that address differing forms of discipleship. The first, Augusto Boal's *Theatre of the Oppressed*, sets the stage and includes variations of development for theatre artists, which has parallels within the church. To complement his work, I include Shannon Craigo-Snell's *The Empty*

27. Manneh, "Lectio Divina."
28. Johnston et al., *Deep Focus*, 127.
29. Johnston et al., *Deep Focus*, 128.

Church, which draws heavily on Brook's *The Empty Space*. Finally, I engage with *Theatrical Theology*, a collection of writings from authors who see the arts as a means of enacting justice in our world, and Vander Lugt's *Living Theodrama*, which provides a means of engaging with Scripture for embodied ethics and discipleship.

Liturgy, the work of the people, is one method of discipleship. According to Craigo-Snell in *The Empty Church*, "Christian liturgy is the performance that forms us as fit players in the ongoing drama of salvation."[30] If worship is one way that we are discipled as followers of Christ, then we must consider how to bring about a method of discipleship absent of a traditional worship gathering, one in which is created a desire to grow deeper in relationship with Jesus.

I propose that most theatre people are motivated by giving voice to oppressed and marginalized people. They are also familiar with development as actors and theatre artists. Therefore, discipleship must be an embodied process that brings about justice. Both Craigo-Snell and Boal speak of the importance of embodiment in the discipleship process, albeit for differing reasons. Craigo-Snell suggests that because we engage all our senses in Christian worship, it is an embodied experience that goes beyond just praising God, but includes using our arms, legs, eyes, noses, and voices as one.[31] This can be witnessed in many faith traditions and can include the acts of kneeling, smelling incense, raising arms in worship, singing music, and visually engaging stained glass windows.

Boal, in *Theatre of the Oppressed*, delineates his methodology of discipling actors, including embodiment. Boal's system for actor transformation consists of four stages, two of which deal with embodiment. They are: (1) knowing the body, (2) making the body expressive, (3) the theatre as language, and (4) the theatre as discourse.[32] An important key to growing in both church and theatre is embodiment as a form of communication. It is described as a cyclical process by Vander Lugt in *Living Theodrama*: "What

---

30. Craigo-Snell, *Empty Church*, 37.

31. Craigo-Snell, *Empty Church*, 23.

32. Boal, *Theatre of the Oppressed*, 126.

constitutes the theatrical process, therefore, is the unending and mutually dependent movement from formation to performance and from performance to formation."[33] Sacred acts inform our faith and our humanity, whether they are liturgical or theatrical.

To draw the parallel to worship as discipleship in a manner that is accessible to the theatre, I focus on three elements of Christian worship that can be extrapolated into the theatre community: communion, Scripture, and worship as service or action.

Our fledgling community of theatre artists on a journey toward God are oriented around the table as gathering space. According to Peter Heltzel in engagement with Boal's work, "The collective work of liturgy enacts communion among those who are participants. Communion is the context for engendering love, justice, and truth among the gathered people of God, especially the poor and oppressed."[34] Creating space for communion around the table is the first step in discipleship: equality is recognized, people are known, and voices are heard. Just as with the Lord's Supper as enacted in corporate worship gatherings, these communal meals give voice to those that are oppressed, or are allies to the oppressed, prayers are offered for the same, and those that gather are strengthened and encouraged.

Scripture has been described as a script by Craigo-Snell,[35] but I believe that Vander Lugt is closer to the truth when describing Scripture as a transcript or prescript, especially in the context of discipleship in the theatre community. The following, from his *Living Theodrama*, is lengthy, but is the best description of this concept:

> Imagine a playwright (God the Father) who has a comprehensive plan for a play, but guides certain writers in transcribing a long series of improvised performances in interaction with his own performance (the theodrama). He does not record every work and action, but only those events, interactions, and explanatory notes that

33. Vander Lugt, *Living Theodrama*, 29.

34. Heltzel, "Church as a Theatre," 254.

35. Craigo-Snell, *Empty Church*, 22.

contribute to a cohesive story (the Old Testament). These transcriptions are taken up by another group of actors (disciples of Jesus) with the task of improvising creatively and consistently with these earlier performances as interpreted and enacted by the playwright himself performing the lead role (Jesus). Later, the playwright also includes letters from various assistant directors (Paul, Peter, John, and so on) to their companies (churches) that suggest more faithful and creative ways of performing in various situations as guided by the producer (Holy Spirit). In the end, the resource given to actors today is not a script per se but a collection of adapted performance transcriptions serving as prescriptions for further performance (the Christian Scriptures). Some of these transcriptions even include predictions of how the play will end (prophecy), so the actors are required to reincorporate by memory what is transcribed while pre-incorporating with hope and imagination elements from the ending.[36]

With this understanding of Scripture as transcript and prescript, we can foster an understanding of how to move forward without legalistic expectations on those that are joining the Company. The term *company* is described by Vander Lugt as the church: a company of many companies.[37] In *Theatrical Theology*, Carter and Wells affirm this view. In describing Scripture, they write, "It was a script for performance, a rallying cry for mission, a tirade seeking repentance, and a chorus of comfort."[38] Carter and Wells conclude that the Bible is not fundamentally a text, but rather a drama: a drama with a script, but a drama that is rehearsed and improvised anew in each setting, in each telling.[39] The concept of improvisation allows us to look at Scripture with fresh eyes depending on the context in which we find ourselves. Improvisation includes the concept of allowing or blocking: the actor can receive from another actor or shut down dialogue depending on their choice.

36. Vander Lugt, *Living Theodrama*, 94.

37. Vander Lugt, *Living Theodrama*, 124.

38. Carter and Wells, "Holy Theatre," 224.

39. Carter and Wells, "Holy Theatre," 227.

Therefore, improvisation brings us to a place where we can say yes to LGBTQ+ individuals without blocking their access.

With the pre-script and transcript in hand, the company is called to action. Heltzel challenges, "Theatre should add a log to the fire of the revolution for radical social change."[40] What we do beyond our time of gathering is worship-in-action. To gauge whether our company members are growing in their understanding of Christian faith, we need to look at their embodiment of the topics they have been engaging with during our gathering times. One unifying concept amongst theatre artists is the desire to enact social justice. It is the linchpin that connects their goals and passions with those of Jesus. According to Heltzel, "Drawing inspiration from the Theodrama of Scripture, we need to imagine new ways to express our prophetic theology dramatically."[41] Theatre artists have no problem with *act-ion*. The goal is to connect the heart and words of Jesus to something that they can enact in their communities. As Boal states, "I believe that all the truly revolutionary theatrical groups should transfer to the people the means of production in the theater so that the people themselves can utilize them. The theater is a weapon, and it is the people who should wield it."[42] This parallels discipleship in that the traditional church transfers knowledge to the people, and they, empowered by the Holy Spirit, utilize what they have learned to expand the reign of Christ in their communities. In the same way, our theatre community is learning how to enact social justice using the inspiration received from the pre-script and transcript of Scripture to change their communities through social justice performances. Theatre is a rehearsal for the revolution,[43] and our theatre company is rehearsing to be part of it. "Sometimes drama is necessary to capture the imagination of the ruling powers of our cities and nations."[44] Agency is released in theatre artists as they are empowered to use

40. Heltzel, "Church as a Theatre," 245.
41. Heltzel, "Church as a Theatre," 243.
42. Boal, *Theatre of the Oppressed*, 122.
43. Boal, *Theatre of the Oppressed*, 122.
44. Heltzel, "Church as a Theatre," 243.

their talent to speak to power and impact their communities. Not only can they be creatives and artists, but they can also take on the role of prophet.

God's presence is abundantly available to be experienced outside of a traditional Sunday morning gathering and is being recognized in community within this new church expression. Theatre artists might not have theologically rich terms for what they have experienced through the performative arts, either by watching or performing, but they affirm divine encounters. Our goal should be to curate those pieces, those experiences, that continue to make room for further transcendent encounters. Through communion, encountering the words of Jesus, and opportunities to prophetically perform, theatre artists will be actively engaged in righting social inequities and bringing about justice in their communities. Out of this fresh soil, a church of theatre artists is emerging, and community is being built.

Chapter 3

Extending the Table

In CHAPTER 3 I lay a theological foundation for church planting within the theatre community. I will begin by developing the theological framework of church planting itself through Jesus' commission to believers and Paul's understanding of the marketplace of thought in Athens. Secondly I develop a theology of the extended and hospitable table, and the inclusive community that gathers around it. Finally, I will place Pentecostal and Queer theology in dialogue to present a means to welcome the LGBTQ+ community into full fellowship at the table and within the body of Christ.

THE GREAT COMMISSION AND CHURCH PLANTING

Turning to the words of Jesus must be the first thing to do when considering the biblical call to all believers to "Go" (Matt 28:20). As recorded in Matthew's Gospel, Jesus tells the disciples, "All authority in heaven and on earth has been given to me. Go therefore and make disciples of all nations, baptizing them in the name of the Father and of the Son and of the Holy Spirit, teaching them to observe all that I have commanded you. And behold, I am with you always, to the end of the age" (Matt 28:18–20).[1] This passage is often used as a basis to support missions—the literal going to other geographic areas in order to share the gospel. It can also speak to the need to church plant in our own backyard if people are not yet part of the Christian faith community. The Greek word ἔθνη, which is translated in the ESV passage above as *nations*, refers to those considered gentiles. It is used in that context fifty-two times in the New Testament. According to the *Lexham Bible Dictionary*, this same word refers to "Groups of people linked by kinship, land, culture, or government."[2] The theatre community is one such people group—linked by kinship and culture.

An alternate Great Commission text, as recorded by Luke, states that we are to be Christ's witnesses (Luke 24:46–48) after which Christ promises the Holy Spirit. This commission comes full circle at the outpouring of the Holy Spirit as Luke reaffirms this same call in Acts 1:8. The Greek word translated as witness is μάρτυς, which is more frequently associated with public testimony. According to Aubrey Malphurs, "The savior didn't want the church to be passive. They weren't to wait for people to come to them; they were to be proactive and go after people. In fact, they were to be out in the community rubbing shoulders with the people who lived there."[3] No longer are we able to expect that just by opening the doors of a church that people will come in. We must be witnesses to Christ. Kevin J. Vanhoozer writes that Jesus' identity and role came together in his unique mission; similarly, our identities and roles merge together too, in the notion of witness.[4] Quoting Augustine, Vanhoozer continues, "One's pattern of behavior can be a kind of 'eloquence,' a lived sermon."[5] It is important to identify to whom we have been called, individually and collectively. A lived

---

1. All Scripture quoted is from the English Standard Version, unless otherwise noted.

2. Durst, "Nations."

3. Malphurs, *Nuts and Bolts*, 89.

4. Vanhoozer, *Drama of Doctrine*, 397.

5. Vanhoozer, *Drama of Doctrine*, 397.

sermon is only possible if we are living our faith in full view of those to whom God has called us.

THE PAULINE MODEL IN THE MARKETPLACE

There is something quite theatrical about Paul's addressing of the people in Athens. After having taken the time to learn about the Athenian people and their culture, he stands up in the middle of the marketplace and gathers an audience. He heralds the townspeople to gather so that he can share the gospel in a way that they can understand. Paul speaks of an unknown God, referring to a piece of art within the city. He explains his methodology in his first letter to the Corinthians by stating that "I have become all things to all people, that by all means I might save some" (1 Cor 9:22). This statement of Paul's, according to Vanhoozer, makes the charter declaration for viewing the church as interactive theatre.[6] Interactive theatre allows for performer and audience to become woven together to tell the story. No longer is there a separation between performer (Paul) and the audience (the people of Athens), but rather they are together experiencing the gospel story through Paul's words and their art.

Furthermore, Vanhoozer then continues to expound this analogy by highlighting the historical significance. As he states, "This Pauline principle became a frequent point of appeal by 16th-century thinkers who were concerned that the church's teaching be adapted to the ignorant as well as the learned."[7] Bringing it into the contemporary context, Vanhoozer writes: "It is precisely because the church must react to the changing needs of society in the world that, in seeking to be 'all things to all people,' it must be interactive theater."[8] In traditional theatre, the audience comes to the stage. In interactive theatre, we are now being called out to the marketplace. We must embody the gospel in such a way as to interact with our audiences in their contexts.

6. Vanhoozer, *Drama of Doctrine*, 414.

7. Vanhoozer, *Drama of Doctrine*, 414.

8. Vanhoozer, *Drama of Doctrine*, 415.

One such approach, according to Vander Lugt and using a theatre analogy, is the concept of experimental church, where the fourth wall is broken down and mission is lived out with the audience.[9] He goes on to explain that the mission of the church is to invite the audience, those who are strangers to the company, to join the performance as guests and eventually to share the same faith.[10] Reiterating Paul's personal missional strategy of becoming all things to all people, Vanhoozer reminds us that "in the interactive theater of the gospel, however, *all* the world's a stage, and *everyone* is a potential guest."[11] Our mission, which is the same as Paul and the other early followers of Jesus, is to enact culturally fitting performances in order to be faithful witnesses to God and his gospel.[12] I propose that the table is where this best happens for an experimental church. The table allows for communion in a space where all are welcome and equal.

HOSPITALITY—EXTENDING THE TABLE AND ENLARGING THE TENT

My goal in this section is to present a theological argument to widen our welcome to those on the outside: theatrical creatives as well as those from the LGBTQ+ community. The table is the place where it can happen.

Earlier I suggested that there has been an historical divide between the theatrical community and the church. According to Gerardus Van Der Leeuw, "The conflict between Church and theater began a long time ago and still continues today."[13] He writes:

> The opposition of the Christian Church to the theater has grounds which are basically historical. In the historical conflict, there is a good measure of irony. We do not

9. Vander Lugt, *Living Theodrama*, 165.

10. Vander Lugt, *Living Theodrama*, 167.

11. Vanhoozer, *Drama of Doctrine*, 416.

12. Vander Lugt, *Living Theodrama*, 192.

13. Van Der Leeuw, *Sacred and Profane Beauty*, 97.

see theater and religion, but two different religions, one against another: the ancient fertility religion of the *sager ludus*, with its candor and sexual symbols, and the new ascetic religion of Christendom. The theater must pay for its fidelity to the ancient primitive religious forms with the hostility of the new religions.[14]

That is but one version of the tension between church and theatre. Vander Lugt begins his work on *Living Theodrama* with this overview of the historical nature of the tension:

> Two opposing currents run deeply in the Christian tradition: the anti-theatrical prejudice and the intrinsic theatricality of faith. The former appeared as footnotes to Plato, whether as ontological objection to imitative representation or ethical disapproval of arousing the passions. Equally dismissive was the Puritan and later fundamentalist perspective that theatre is an epicenter of evil, existing merely for base entertainment. Although many Christians today endorse neither Platonic nor Puritan prejudices against theatre, the lingering effects still permeate everyday parlance.[15]

I can confirm that within my own denomination there are those that still believe that playing cards, acting, and dancing are outside the realm of righteousness for a Christian. It is true that artists are a product of the division of our culture. They do not fit into our social order, there is nothing there for them.[16] Given the church's call to the ministry of reconciliation (2 Cor 5:19), it is the church's responsibility to create generative spaces where this divide can be bridged and healed.

The irony of the historical divide is this: creatives, as a reflection of their Creator, express the beauty of holiness through their art and should be welcomed rather than ostracized. Theatre artists model this welcome every time they perform: the audience, who are those on the perimeter and outside, are welcomed into the

---

14. Van Der Leeuw, *Sacred and Profane Beauty*, 97.

15. Vander Lugt, *Living Theodrama*, 1.

16. Van Der Leeuw, *Sacred and Profane Beauty*, 271.

intimacy of the art each time it is performed. This art, according to Van Der Leeuw, is the basis of all art and the basis of all humanity, because it is one of the most noble forms of the great human art of comprehension, of placing one's self "inside another," which is the secret of forgiveness and love.[17] The parallel to the church is this: "The communal and relational context of theodramatic performance extends beyond the company of actors to include the audience: those outside the company who are not committed to participating in the theodrama as presented in Scripture."[18] Therefore, as Christ-followers, it is imperative that we extend the table to include those from the theatre community without hesitation.

It is equally important to include members of the LGBTQ+ community. I will soon address the theological issues of this stance, but for now I would like to include the LGBTQ+ community as we consider extending the table, as both the LGBTQ+ community and the theatre community have historically been ostracized from the church and pushed to the margins.[19] Fujimura refers to those on the outside of the dominant culture as *mearcstapas*, using a word from the Old English that means border walkers or border stalkers. In the tribal realities of earlier times, these were individuals who lived on the edges of their groups, going in and out of the permeable borders, sometimes bringing back news to the tribe.[20] Artists, as people on the margins, are able to view the culture that is proximate to their location. By ostracizing artists in the past, we lost a prophetic voice in our congregations. It is possible that we have so reduced the gift of prophecy to words only that we have lost the prophetic edge of dance, art, music, and theatre. Fujimura states that for a *mearcstapa* to come to full maturity, they need not only friendship, but deliberate cultivation in community.[21] The best way to foster this community and deepen friendships is through intentional table gatherings.

17. Van Der Leeuw, *Sacred and Profane Beauty*, 102.

18. Vander Lugt, *Living Theodrama*, 10.

19. Fujimura, *Culture Care*, 58.

20. Fujimura, *Culture Care*, 58.

21. Fujimura, *Culture Care*, 60.

Communion at the table has been a foundation of the Christian faith since the time of Jesus himself. Jesus was a beautiful model of intentional relationship fostered around tables and shared meals. I present a theology of the table based on the historical practice of the Lord's Supper as well as an eschatological imagining of this same table. According to Jürgen Moltmann, "Just as the Lord's supper is a sign of fellowship and not of division, so the corresponding theology will have to present what is in common and not what divides."[22] A table gathering as proposed must leave room for disagreement amid a shared love of theatre. The theatre community does include those that love theatre, but that is the beginning and the end of expected shared traits. It is an eclectic gathering of many different types of people. These differences could foster negativity if not handled well with grace and an openness to differing opinions.

No one need be sanctified before coming to the table. When Jesus shared time around the table with the disciples, it was not an exclusive meal enjoyed by the righteous. It was a gathering of Jesus' friends, who were on mission with him.[23] Their diversity is celebrated as they are gathered. In the same way, we are called to invite those who are on the margins to the table, celebrating their diversity and respecting their place on the journey, Christ-follower or not. This new covenant and new fellowship are in tendency universal, all-embracing, and exclusive of no one; they are open to the world because they point to the banquet of the nations.[24] The nations are every tribe and tongue, which includes theatre artists and gay Christians in full fellowship at the table.

The Lord's table and communion can bring reconciliation and awareness of the oppressed, which includes those on the margins such as the LGBTQ+ community and theatre artists. According to Moltmann, "Anyone who celebrates the Lord's supper in a world of hunger and oppression does so in complete solidarity with the sufferings and hopes of all men, because he believes that the Messiah

22. Moltmann, *Church in the Power*, 245.

23. Moltmann, *Church in the Power*, 249.

24. Moltmann, *Church in the Power*, 252.

invites all men to his table and because he hopes that they will all sit at table with him."[25] Rather than being an exclusive table, it is an inclusive table and needs to be the center of the gathering. Moltmann also states that "the fellowship of the table cannot be restricted to people who are 'faithful to the church,' or to the 'inner circle' of the community."[26] What a wonderful freedom to include those that are far from God—and those that have been restricted access to God due to their creativeness or their sexual orientation.

The table is where healing can happen. In *Healing Our Broken Humanity*, Grace Ji-Sun Kim and Graham Hill present nine practices for revitalizing the modern church, all of which lean into a vision of a new humanity. According to the authors, "Jesus calls us to reimagine the church as the new humanity in Jesus Christ."[27] Out of the nine practices, the one that is most applicable here is to reactivate hospitality. According to Kim and Hill, these new humanity churches "embrace the diversity of the body of Christ. They embrace this fully, not in a partial or tokenistic way. They welcome diversity in its many forms. They grasp the importance of ethnic, linguistic, cultural, gender, racial, socioeconomic, and theological diversity."[28] It is important to recognize that theological diversity might be required in order to have true welcoming diversity that includes those in the LGBTQ+ community. Holding these differences in tension while respecting and loving each other is a mark of the presence of Jesus amid those that differ. As Kim and Hill state, "all that incredible diversity has a single, authentic point of unity: Jesus Christ."[29] Where Christ is the head and host, unity at the table is possible.

In too many situations, the laws and codes of people have superseded the grace of Christ. Our churches are filled with rules on who can serve at table, who is welcome at table, and who cannot even approach. If we take Jesus as our guide, we will witness one

25. Moltmann, *Church in the Power*, 258.

26. Moltmann, *Church in the Power*, 259.

27. Kim and Hill, *Healing Our Broken Humanity*, 21.

28. Kim and Hill, *Healing Our Broken Humanity*, 110.

29. Kim and Hill, *Healing Our Broken Humanity*, 111.

who ate with outsiders, was open in welcome, and did not expect change or transformation before welcoming anyone to join in the meal. Kim and Hill, quoting Henri J. M. Nouwen, write, "Hospitality, therefore, means primarily the creation of a free space where the stranger can enter and become friend instead of an enemy. Hospitality is not to change people, but to offer them space where change can take place."[30] I want to be clear that the change I am addressing and advocating is not changing from gay to straight, but rather change from one who does not know Jesus to one who does.

In 1 Corinthians 11, Paul instructs the church at Corinth in regard to the Lord's Supper. He states that "For as often as you eat this bread and drink the cup, you proclaim the Lord's death until he comes." The gathering of the body of Christ around the table is an act of remembrance as well as a prophetic act. We are called to continue the practice until Jesus returns. Radical hospitality at the table is also a prophetic act. "We welcome people into our homes and lives and lands in anticipation of the home and the age to come."[31] A truly diverse and welcoming community gathered around the table is an image of the great heavenly feast, where Christ is the head.

In moving into the final section of this chapter, it is important to recognize the work of C. S. Lewis in helping to expand the way that one can think about theology in our context. Lewis coined the term *transposition*, which is a striking example of rendering the same in the different.[32] In music, in order to accommodate a singer or musician, it is possible to transpose pieces of music from one key to another key; basically creating a different version of the same art, but one that is more accessible than the original. According to Vanhoozer, "Dramatic transposition, like its musical counterpart, is a matter of preserving the same melodic line and harmonic configuration, though in a different key, where 'melody' is the main line of action and 'harmony' the broader context that

---

30. Kim and Hill, *Healing Our Broken Humanity*, 119.

31. Kim and Hill, *Healing Our Broken Humanity*, 121.

32. Vanhoozer, *Drama of Doctrine*, 254.

gives the melody its specific meaning."[33] We just need to learn how to transpose the beauty of the gospel into a key that enables those that are far from God, those on the margins, to be able to sing.

Our job is to transpose the gospel so that all may hear as well as sing. Then we are to make room for whosoever will to come under the tent; all the while adding inserts into our old dining room table so that there is room for all. As Nadia Bolz-Weber writes,

> This desire to learn what the faith is from those who have lived it in the face of being told they are not welcome or worthy is far more than "inclusion." Actually, inclusion isn't the right word at all, because it sounds like in our niceness and virtue we are allowing "them" to join "us"—like we are musing another group of people to be worthy of inclusion in a tent that we don't own. I can only look at the seemingly limited space under the tent and think either it's my job to change people so they fit or it's my job to extend the roof so that they fit. Either way, it's misguided because it's not my tent. It's God's tent.[34]

The beauty of this welcoming table and tent is that my Pentecostal brothers and sisters and my LGBTQ+ family can sit at the same table. It will take making room for disagreements and wrestling with those disagreements, but there can be room for compromise and shared understanding.

PENTECOSTAL AND QUEER THEOLOGY—OUR COMMON GROUND

As mentioned earlier, I have my feet firmly planted between two worlds: the more conservative Assemblies of God, and the more progressive LGBTQ+-affirming community of theatre artists. It is my goal to create space for those in the LGBTQ+ community as fully included members of Christ's church. Although there are many more liberal mainline denominations that have moved toward a more open and affirming stance, the Assemblies of God

33. Vanhoozer, *Drama of Doctrine*, 254.
34. Bolz-Weber, *Pastrix*, 94.

has yet to move in that direction. It is possible that it never will, but the unique distinctives of Pentecostal denominations, like the Assemblies of God, could be life-changing for the LGBTQ+ community. Therefore, I focus on the work of the Holy Spirit in the lives of believers and the church first to find possible common ground. I then propose three areas that can be our foundation for moving forward.

Historically, the church has been able to make marked changes in the way it has approached people considered outside the realm of God's grace, beginning with the Jerusalem council. As Pentecostal author Stanley M. Horton writes, "The question had arisen: How could the Jewish believers maintain fellowship with Gentile Christians that were not circumcised, who ate non-kosher food, and who came out of the highly immoral Greek culture of the day?"[35] The council members were able to come to an agreement whereby gentiles were included fully in the life of the church, with a few stipulations. Horton goes on to say, "The qualities they needed in order to work together and bear testimony by their lives were not ordinary graces, but the fruit of the Spirit."[36] David P. Gushee concurs saying, "It's really important to remind people that the church has gotten some key things wrong before, has repented, and has recovered to enter a more faithful path of discipleship. We did it on slavery, race, and anti-Semitism. We can do it now."[37] As a gentile, female, ordained minister of the gospel who has benefitted from previous resolved disagreements, I propose that it is time for another council of sorts in which we should consider how to include LGBTQ+ Christians in full fellowship. Those same fruits of the Spirit made evident in the lives of the early church can move in such a way that we can find common ground to move forward once again.

Horton makes the point that "Pentecostals stand firm at the point that marks off Bible-believers from so-called liberals. The line of demarcation is not the acceptance simply of the Virgin

35. Horton, *What the Bible Says*, 9.

36. Horton, *What the Bible Says*, 12.

37. Gushee, *Changing Our Mind*, 141.

Birth, the Cross, or the Resurrection. It is rather the supernatural itself."[38] This statement highlights the fact that theology is not the only element that might separate different expressions of Christ's church, but the existence of the supernatural, specifically the supernatural as experienced through the Holy Spirit. This is why I believe it is so important that the Assemblies of God and other more conservative Pentecostal denominations consider full inclusion of the LGBTQ+ community: the work of the Holy Spirit.

The existence of the supernatural is life-changing and should not be restricted but made available to all those who are seeking an encounter with God. As Fujimura writes, "The Holy Spirit is active at the margins of our churches, drawing people in. When we hold our gate shut, we not only starve our own sheep but our pursuit of safety becomes a barrier to entry for Jesus' other sheep."[39] The concept of starving our own sheep is critical, because the church is diminished when creatives from the LGBTQ+ community are not welcomed within the church's gates. Patrick S. Cheng, affirming the creativity and reflection of the Creator of LGBTQ+ people, states that:

> Many LGBT people are actively engaged in acts of creation on a daily basis—whether it is playing music, singing, dancing, acting, painting, writing poetry, or even doing theology. Indeed, it is not an exaggeration to say that the performing arts community, including the church musician community, would have been greatly impoverished without the gifts and contributions of queer people through the centuries.[40]

The church would be richer with the presence of theatrical LGBTQ+ people. With the LGBTQ+ community's love of the dramatic and ability to story-tell powerful narratives, they would be a blessing to Christ's church. The Holy Spirit is drawing them in; we should not lean on the door to keep it shut, but rather fling wide the gates to allow the move of the Holy Spirit in our midst.

38. Horton, *What the Bible Says*, 13.

39. Fujimura, *Culture Care*, 91.

40. Cheng, *Radical Love*, chap. 3.

There are those that might counter by saying that LGBTQ+ people are welcome in their conservative churches. Welcomed is not full inclusion and comes with stipulations of change. Using the sheepfold analogy, these churches, filled with white-fleeced sheep, would welcome the rainbow-fleeced sheep if only they would bleach their wool, rather than celebrate the beauty of the rainbow-colored fleece and how it augments the beauty of the sheepfold.

Although I realize that finding common ground might be difficult, it is not impossible. We must begin somewhere because lives and souls are at stake. Although there is a great chasm between Pentecostal/conservative theology and Queer theology, it is necessary to start to find the kite strings that will yield a bridge in the future.[41] Therefore, I propose that we commit to be pastoral and agree to do no harm to those that God is drawing into our midst. Even for those that hold to a more conservative doctrine, it is possible to commit to this first level of common ground. I suggest three areas in which we can make strides toward this goal: rein in our behavior and vocabulary, minister to the youth in our congregations, and develop an openness and respect for various hermeneutics.

The first commitment to do no harm begins with our behavior and vocabulary. Vanhoozer states that "Theology is charged with helping the church adopt a language that will communicate the gospel in new contexts and a life that will embody the gospel in new contexts."[42] If the gospel is truly good news then our vocabulary must extend that good news to LGBTQ+ people that have been rejected by those in the church. Our language and our behavior needs to be redeemed as a reflection of our Redeemer.

As David P. Gushee writes:

> [I]t is increasingly agreed, even on the traditionalist Christian side: gay people exist. It is wrong to call them names or use slurs about them. Their relationships should not be criminalized. They should not be discriminated

---

41. This is a reference to the first suspension bridge built across the Niagara River.

42. Vanhoozer, *Drama of Doctrine*, 73.

against in employment, housing and public accommodation. They should not be bullied. They should never have to be afraid of violence as they go about their daily lives. They should not be blamed for American security problems or social ills. They should not be stigmatized or treated with contempt. There should be no space in church life or culture for their dehumanization and mistreatment.[43]

This might seem obvious at first blush, but much of what has been done in the name of following Christ has been anything but reflective of the heart of Christ. Fighting against gay marriage, refusing to serve gay customers, and picketing gay events are just three examples that barely reveal the tip of the iceberg. We must reduce the hateful rhetoric that defines the loudest voices from evangelicalism in our time.

One of the first ways to do better and to diminish this culture of dehumanization within the church is by eliminating the word *sin* in respect to LGBTQ+ people. I address this later in this chapter, but for now, it is important to understand just how painful the word *sin* can be. According to Cheng:

> Sin is not just a matter of abstract debate for LGBT people. Sin-talk has justified the persecution, imprisonment, torture, and even execution of LGBT people by governments around the world. Sin-talk has resulted in suicides by young people and adults who are condemned by their families, communities, and churches for their sexualities and gender identities. Sin-talk is also at the heart of discredited attempts at changing sexual and gender identities through "ex-gay" or reparative therapy that purports to "pray away the gay."[44]

Even if one were to hold to the belief that homosexuality is sin, there ultimately is an unpublished hierarchy of sin that exists. The same people that would fight against gay marriage and refuse to serve homosexuals would not make the effort to stop gossips from

43. Gushee, *Changing Our Mind*, 32.
44. Cheng, *From Sin*, 6.

marrying or refuse to serve someone with an anger issue. The hierarchy of sin that exists has the quality of hypocrisy and must be eliminated. We can omit our hypocrisy by removing the word *sin* from our dialogue when it comes to homosexuality.

As to the ex-gay therapies that Cheng mentions, there are theological conservatives that celebrate the stories of men and women that have left the gay lifestyle or have been delivered from homosexuality. Theological conservatives are ignoring the painful effects of these same ministries as well as the long-term failure of the same. The efforts of organizations that offer conversion therapies hoping that prayer will remove one's sexual orientation are notably detrimental to LGBTQ+ people. Gushee highlights many of these organizations, as well as leading psychiatric organizations that warn against conversion or reparative therapies, concluding that "It is hard to see how responsible Christian ministries can any longer offer, or refer to, sexual-orientation-change therapy."[45] Gay Christians need to find sanctuary within our churches, not damaging theologies and discrimination. The only time prayer should be used as a weapon is in dealing with the demonic or in spiritual battles.

The second area of commitment to do no harm involves the youngest of our families—the least of these (Matt 25:40). Anti-LGBTQ+ rhetoric has been severely detrimental to the youth of our churches and families. According to Gushee,

> Without doctrinal change, we are still telling LGBTQ kids that their sexuality is not just not right, but sinful, broken or disordered in a way that straight kids' sexuality is not. We are still telling them that they can never have an adult sexual or romantic relationship that could please God or be blessed by the church. We are still very likely telling them that they will be treated as second class citizens when it comes to serving and leading the church. We are "welcoming" them, maybe, but not on

---

45. Gushee, *Changing Our Mind*, 27.

equal terms with their peers, which is a "welcome" not many of the rest of us would accept.[46]

We cannot ignore how the influence of church teaching on this matter has affected the acceptance and safety of LGBTQ+ youth. Not only are the attitudes of their peers affected negatively, impacting their relationships, LGBTQ+ youth are also subject to self-defeating attitudes in response to conservative theological stances.

According to the Trevor Project, the following statistics have been reported as recently as 2022:

- 45 percent of LGBTQ youth seriously considered attempting suicide in the past year. Whereas youth who live in a community that is accepting of LGBTQ people reported significantly lower rates of attempted suicide than those who do not.

- 14 percent of LGBTQ youth attempted suicide in the past year. The rate is 20 percent for transgender youth.

- 36 percent of LGBTQ youth reported that they have been physically threatened or harmed due to either their sexual orientation or gender identity.

- 73 percent of LGBTQ youth reported that they have experienced discrimination based on their sexual orientation or gender identity at least once in their lifetime.[47]

These statistics involve responses to negative and aggressive behavior directed to LGBTQ+ youth because of their sexual orientation or gender identity.

We can also see that supporting and loving communities do make a difference to LGBTQ+ youth. Outside of their families, these loving, supportive communities should include the church. Instead, churches continue to promote conversion therapies for LGBTQ+ youth. According to this same survey, 17 percent of LGBTQ youth report being threatened with or subjected to conversion therapy. As Amit Paley states, "Conversion therapy has been

46. Gushee, *Changing Our Mind*, 171.

47. Trevor Project, "2022 National Survey."

consistently associated with negative mental health outcomes and greater risk for suicide. That's why this so-called 'therapy' is widely opposed by all major medical and mental organizations."[48] In other studies it has been found that:

- Rates of attempted suicide by LGBTQ young people whose parents and caregivers tried to change their sexual orientation were more than double (48 percent) the rate for LGBTQ young people who reported no conversion attempts (22 percent).

- Levels of depression in LGBTQ young adults were more than double (33 percent) for LGBTQ young people whose parents tried to change their sexual orientation compared with levels for those who reported no conversion experiences (16 percent); the levels were more than triple (52 percent) for LGBTQ young people who reported both home-based efforts to change their sexual orientation by parents and external SOCE [sexual orientation change efforts] by therapists and religious leaders.[49]

The best course of action is to discontinue conversion therapy across the board. Not only is it discredited by major medical and mental health organizations, it is increasing the suicide rate amongst LGBTQ+ young people. If we can commit to support and love these young people without the negativity of sin-talk and conversion therapy, we will have made great strides toward working toward a more loving and Christlike environment within our churches.

The third and final area in which we can find common ground and possible agreement is in hermeneutics. This might seem the place where there is the least likelihood of agreement, but if we can get to a place where we humbly accept that none of us is the sole arbiter of truth, then we can work together to strive toward a more loving response.

48. Trevor Project, "2022 National Survey."
49. Glassgold and Ryan, "Role of Families," 93.

This final section does not address theological interpretation of specific verses in the Bible that are used by non-affirming Christians to qualify homosexuality as sin. Many other authors have done due diligence in addressing these verses so that we have much to consider when it comes to affirming and including LGBTQ+ people within our congregations.[50] I have chosen to address hermeneutic plurality in the Appendix. Rather, this concluding section lays out the foundation of mutual respect and understanding, in hopes of future dialogue.

We must first agree that we serve a God that is unfathomable. Every facet of God and God's intent for us as God's creation is not possibly known to us in our frailty and limited ability as humans. God has provided Scripture to help us ascertain God's character as well as God's will for us personally and corporately. Yet, there are limitations. Using a theatrical analogy, Vander Lugt proposes, "As a diverse collection of literature written by a variety of authors in different cultures, scripture paints an elusive and partial picture of God's intentions as playwright, leaving many questions unanswered."[51] He goes on to write, "Although some clear principles do emerge from scripture, it is not primarily a textbook for providing black-and-white answers to contemporary conundrums, which is why every other dimension—trinitarian, traditional, ecclesial, missional, and contextual—is necessary for disponible formation and fitting performance."[52] This partial picture allows us to admit that we do not have all the answers and no one denomination or theological viewpoint is without fault.

The tension between holding fast to one's theological viewpoint and allowing for different voices exists even within the same

50. Please refer to Marin, *Love is an Orientation*. Mr. Marin might not come as far on the issue as I do, but he does a wonderful job at changing the dialogue and striving toward understanding from the side of the oppressed. See also Vine, *God and the Gay Christian*, and Gushee, *Changing Our Mind*.

51. Vander Lugt, *Living Theodrama*, 66.

52. Vander Lugt, *Living Theodrama*, 112. I note the unusual word *disponible*. According to *Merriam-Webster*, *disponible* means "capable of being placed, arranged, or disposed of as one wishes: available."

publication. In warning against reading Scripture through our personal experience, Vanhoozer writes:

> For example, the suggestion that "doctrinal dramas be tested in the concrete lives of women" risks making a particular kind of human experience a touchstone for what is doctrinally acceptable and hence a de facto authority. Like other "advocacy theologies" that attempt to do theology from the perspective of the experience of a particular social or gender or racial group, this procedure mistakenly locates Christian identity other than where it belongs, namely "in Christ."[53]

Although I strongly agree with Vanhoozer that our identity needs to be firmly rooted in Christ, I would counter that we have learned and grown much through various theologies such as liberation theology, feminist theology, and Queer theology. Vanhoozer even contradicts himself, affirming diverse theologies, by writing later within the same work, "It is thanks largely to liberation and post modern theology that we have come to appreciate the fact that theologies are not as neutral, nor as removed from the action, as they sometimes seem. Things look different from the perspective of the poor."[54] Specifically things look different from the oppressed. The LGBTQ+ community are members of an oppressed class, and their viewpoints must be considered.

Historically, theology and conservative doctrine have been used to oppress different individuals at different times. Referring to traditional doctrines of sin and grace, Cheng suggests:

> Such doctrines historically have been shaped by men, and they have been used to subjugate and harm women, particularly to the extent that Eve (and, by implication, all women) has been blamed for the fall and original sin. Similarly, African-Americans and other communities of color have been literally enslaved by the biblical narratives about the sin of Ham and curse of Canaan.[55]

53. Vanhoozer, *Drama of Doctrine*, 19.

54. Vanhoozer, *Drama of Doctrine*, 85.

55. Cheng, *From Sin*, xv.

A variety of theological voices are needed to come to a consensus, or at least a starting point, regarding LGBTQ+ inclusion in the church. It is no longer acceptable to believe that only one group of people has the exclusive on truth as expressed in Scripture.

In 1996, Richard B. Hays, then professor of New Testament at Duke, wrestled with the topic of homosexuality when a good friend of his sought his counsel on how to live as a Christian gay man. Although, at that time, he came down firmly that it was not appropriate for homosexual Christians to express their sexuality,[56] he did allow for an open door to possible exploration of this topic moving forward. Hays wrote:

> Only because the new experience of Gentile converts proved *hermeneutically illuminating* of Scripture was the church, over time, able to accept the decision to embrace Gentiles within the fellowship of God's people. This is precisely the step that has not—*or at least not yet* [emphasis mine]—been taken by the advocates of homosexuality in the church. Is it possible for them to re-read the New Testament and show how this development can be understood as a fulfillment of God's design for human sexuality as previously revealed in Scripture? In view of the content of the biblical text summarized [in his chapter on homosexuality], it is difficult to imagine how such an argument could be made.[57]

Almost thirty years later we are the beneficiaries of just how such developments have been made by authors such as Gushee and Vine. The illumination of Scripture that allows for us to consider full inclusion of LGBTQ+ people has been brought to light and it is our choice to consider it or reject it. It is my hope as an affirming pastor that we take the time to seriously consider our stance as Pentecostals when it comes to inclusion of LGBTQ+ individuals.

The unity and witness of the church is at stake. A baseline goal that we should have, as proposed in 1996 by Hays, is this:

56. Hays, *Moral Vision*, 401.

57. Hays, *Moral Vision*, 399. Hays later changed his mind, co-authoring an LGBTQ+-affirming book with his son, an Old Testament scholar. See Hays and Hays, *Widening of God's Mercy*.

> We must find ways to live within the church in a situation of serious moral disagreement while still respecting one another as brothers and sisters in Christ. If the church is going to start practicing the discipline of exclusion from the community, there are other issues far more important than homosexuality where we should begin to draw the line in the dirt: violence and materialism, for example.[58]

Currently today, we have many other issues to work toward as Christ-followers in addition to what Hays suggests: racism, poverty, creation care, and care of the foreigner. Given the research available to us today and beyond as well as hermeneutics that allow for the full inclusion of LGBTQ+ people, it is time to place our focus on those things that have become sidelined as energies have been focused on what has been termed "the gay agenda."

Returning to the arts as this chapter closes, I share a quote from *Deep Focus*. Granted this quote is responding to critical voices regarding a film, but it does resonate when it comes to disparate voices and creating space for them, which is the goal of this chapter and book:

> The church's seeming inability to cultivate these kinds of generative spaces has led to an increasingly fragmented and tribalized notion of Christian community—one comprising isolated echo chambers filled with people who cannot communicate much less commune, with those who do not think, talk, and act exactly as they do. The question then is whether the church will simply continue to echo the wider culture and its politics or whether she will lead the way by modeling a more constructive form of public dialog.[59]

I believe Christ's church must lead the way in this, and that these generative spaces must be created to come to a workable solution to include our LGBTQ+ family members fully in the lives of our churches. We must agree to live in the tension, but not allow the

---

58. Hays, *Moral Vision*, 400.

59. Johnston et al., *Deep Focus*, 198.

tension to overrule us. Rather, we must fully love, fully embrace, and fully welcome and include all whom the Holy Spirit is drawing.

Chapter 4

Creating Dinner Theatre . . . Church?

HOW DINNER THEATRE . . . CHURCH? BEGAN— FOUR FORMATIVE GATHERINGS

Private journal entry, dated December 7, 2021:

> Crucible—twenty incredible people helped to tell a powerful story. It was a bucket-list show and now it's finished. So this group—it's a disparate group of creatives brought together to tell a story. And then what? What makes a community a faith community? Praying for one another? Sharing a meal? Talking about things of faith? I still don't know the next steps, but God continues to allow conversations to happen organically—not by my imposition, but led by those that would not call themselves spiritual. It appears I am a safe ear—a place/person with whom verbal processing can happen. There is a perfect storm happening right now. [List of events.] Not sure what will happen with the church, but COH [City on a Hill] is separate and free to become another avenue of investing in people without the oversight of the AG [Assemblies of God]. Will this actually become something other than a sporadic theatre production? Will it solidify

into a community? And even more, will it coalesce into something where Jesus is center?

This was a catalytic entry, even though I did not recognize it at the time. It took another six months and living through the production of *The Diary of Anne Frank* to make the jump and actively explore what it means to launch a new church expression just for theatre people. As Fujimura states, "A healthy and thriving culture is impossible without the participation of artists and other leaders who are educated intellectually, trained experientially, formed spiritually, and growing morally. Beauty is both a goal and a catalyst for each of these elements."[1] My goal was to create a space for the spiritual growth of theatre artists and *Dinner Theatre . . . Church?* became the means to do it. To reach the largest audience, I made an invitation via Facebook. My initial idea was to host a series of four dinners over the summer as a means of testing the receptiveness of the theatre community. My initial post was the following:

> June 3, 2022: Hello everyone! I hope this finds you well. As you know, I am currently the pastor of a local congregation in Gardner, MA. It is a great group of people that I truly love and am honored to lead.
>
> But the truth is, I am eager to start something new: something that would be home for my theatre community in all their creative fabulousness as well. So I am beginning the process of launching a place for theatre people to gather, enjoy some food, and have discussions about faith—questions, concerns, even disagreements. Like auditions, this is open to all. My hope is that we can create a community—one where we don't have to agree on everything, but where we know we are welcome and loved. And yes, we experience that during our productions, but then we all go our separate ways and lose the connections that were so strong during that season.
>
> I am hosting four dinners throughout this summer—I welcome you to join me at one or all of them. Two will be at my home in Ashby; two will be at our cottage at Camp

1. Fujimura, *Culture Care*, 48.

W in Ashburnham. I have created a Facebook event for these dinners—you may respond to the event itself, or even message me privately if you have any questions. I am eager to share this time with you.

I was strangely anxious about publicly posting after I wrote all of this. I had realized, before posting this, that thinking about doing something and doing it are two very different things. Before I posted the invitation, I could not fail. No one could reject this idea if it were not made public. Once I posted there was no turning back and I waited to see if anyone would attend.

Our first official gathering was on June 20, 2022. There were nine in attendance, including me. Food is central to our gathering time, so we had a potato bar. We gathered in my backyard, shared a meal, and enjoyed a great conversation. I did not have a detailed agenda except for two things: lay down the rules of life (see below) together and hear people's stories. These rules allow us to encounter others just as they are and receive them as a gift, rather than imposing selfish constraints and expectations.[2] The rules of life for *Dinner Theatre . . . Church?* include the following:

- Members are free to say what they believe.

- We exist in a judgement-free zone.

- People are not allowed to correct other people's belief systems.

- It's a safe space to be.

- Nothing that is shared within our gathering can be shared outside of our gathering time.

With those safeguards in place we began by hearing each person's faith story. In confirmation of this next step in gathering, Vander Lugt agrees by stating, "One of the best ways to balance receptivity and confrontation is to share and listen to one another's stories."[3] He goes on to write that "this does not entail, however, that hosts have to agree with everything guests offer, although the

---

2. Vander Lugt, *Living Theodrama*, 118–19.
3. Vander Lugt, *Living Theodrama*, 175.

process of receptive listening opens our eyes to view their ideas as gifts to over-accept."[4] This has been a key concept in our gathering times. The safety that exists to share without fear of retribution or correction has allowed a freedom in discourse that might not otherwise exist.

This first gathering consisted of an eclectic turnout: an Armenian Orthodox, a Baptist woman (whose ex-husband and father of her daughter is gay), someone raised in a Catholic church who departed the day of his confirmation, someone with almost no concept of God who did not attend church except for funerals and weddings, someone raised Catholic who is currently in a Unitarian Universalist church, and someone who was raised and abused in foster care who left the faith but has since returned.

We began at 6:30 in the evening and were still going strong at 8:30, but I closed at that time so people would feel released to leave and invited whoever might want to stay to linger. Some stayed until 10:00. I felt it was a great start to something new. An attendee sent me the following text after we parted company: "I love you friend. Thank you for making me interested in exploring faith."

The next time we met, there were only four of us gathered around the fire. I originally had eight that had planned to attend, but many canceled that day. Initially I was disappointed, but ultimately it became evident that it was a good thing. One person that attended this second evening is quiet and can be overrun by the more vociferous in our gathering. This time he had space and time to process his thoughts.

Unlike the first gathering, this time I was more intentional with our discussion subject. This eventually became known as "mining for a nugget" to foster and propel our discussion. Throughout the first of our meetings, only I mined for the nugget. In this case, it came from *Performing the Sacred*: "Audiences may experience an epiphany at a play, whether that play is consciously 'Christian' or not; God is not limited by our conscious preparation (as artists or audiences). God's spirit enters our lives in the most

---

4. Vander Lugt, *Living Theodrama*, 175.

surprising of places—even in the theater."[5] This was the seed to discuss times where we had transcendent moments, whether in theatre, film, TV, visual art, or in nature. I began the discussion so that they could understand what I was asking them to share. My favorite example is always *Les Misérables*—the moment that the bishop gives Valjean the silver—and how we are called to be better people with the gifts that God gives us, especially God's grace and mercy. My example opened the discussion and all present participated in the discussion. Each person had a unique experience of the transcendent, because, as Robert Johnston clarifies, "Rather than being the possible experience of every person, at all times, everywhere, God's wider revelatory presence is instead the specific experience of people sometimes and on some occasions."[6] Each person shared something unique. Some had experiences outdoors, some in television, some in theatre, some in the movies.

What was most interesting were the examples shared by the quieter individual in our group. His examples all included a character that made a large sacrifice on behalf of others. When I suggested that these characters were possible Christ figures, he had a personal epiphany. He was able to see the connection between the characters that he felt drawn to and Christ's sacrifice on his behalf.

I closed with another nugget drawn from *Performing the Sacred*: "Theatre is a way for us to incarnate our stories, to live with one another in community, and to experience the presence of our fellows and of God. Theatre is a powerful medium."[7] By sharing this quote I was able to draw the parallel between theatre and a church gathering. I was also able to draw the parallels between the overarching narrative of Scripture, the narratives of our own lives, and the narratives within theatre that we can portray.

Our third gathering had eight people—including a few new faces that had not attended before. This allowed for us to review the rules of life as well as allowed people to share their stores if they had not had the chance. We also invited people to share other

5. Johnson and Savidge, *Performing the Sacred*, 50.

6. Johnston, *God's Wider Presence*, 189.

7. Johnson and Savidge, *Performing the Sacred*, 50.

transcendent moments, for those that missed the prior gathering. During this gathering, I was more intentional about adding in some liturgical practices. The first was an invitation to share things for which they were thankful. Each person shared one thing for which they were thankful.

I then shared the nugget for the evening, which was a quote from *Performing the Sacred*:

> While it has been suggested that all art is a performance at some level, we believe that theatre is such a powerful art form because its performative quality embodies three central theological categories that define the nature of human and divine interaction: incarnation, community, and presence. Although other art forms can embody one or two of these qualities, theatre is unique among the arts in its ability to reflect the *imago Dei* in all three ways.[8]

This fostered a discussion around the table regarding those three elements: incarnation, community, and presence. Many beautiful analogies were shared regarding theatre and the church, especially surrounding the concepts of community and presence. The general theme of the commentary from the group centered on how we are present to each other within a cast as well as the audience's presence during performances.

One of the highlighted quotes of the evening was the following from one of the members: "My heart knows you because we both do this thing." A connection exists within the theatre community because of the connection to the art and love of the art form of theatre.

The second liturgical element that I introduced was singing. I did not choose a Christian song but used a secular song by a Christian artist. We sang together, "I Still Haven't Found What I'm Looking For," by U2. It had the same type of effect within this group that singing does in a traditional church gathering. It was able to join people together to share in a song as it would in church—words were sung that were meaningful and the beauty

---

8. Johnson and Savidge, *Performing the Sacred*, 56.

of voices gathered together had a transcendent quality, even if not intended as worship.

The final element I introduced was to ask for any challenges that people have been experiencing. People were forthcoming with their struggles: a new home, the need to focus, constant worry, what next steps someone should take, family stress, the need to connect, requested favor for a meeting, and the desire to reconnect with a child. This allowed me to offer to pray at the conclusion of our gathering. I explained that I pray in the name of Jesus, but it was not necessary for them to do so. We closed and dismissed those that needed to leave, but as in previous times, people lingered to continue our time together.

I received two follow-up texts from members after this gathering. One stated that "I'm so glad to be a part of [*Dinner Theatre . . . Church?*]. I've never had a safe space where I felt like I could explore my relationship with faith and whether I want more, and this has been great." Another woman stated, "You make me feel that my 'way' of having a relationship with God is perfectly OK. There doesn't have to be rules and I just love your way." With this encouragement I began to eagerly anticipate our final gathering of the summer.

Our fourth and final preview gathering (meaning these first four were the foundation for what could be, should we decide to continue) included eight people once again, with some new people joining the gathering. We began by sharing dinner inside my camp cottage, so the conversations were divided up by seating arrangement inside. I also reviewed the rules of life for those that were new to the group. We then moved to the fire circle to begin our discussion in earnest. I have learned that sitting around a fire is conducive to great conversations. Maybe it provides an element of focus, but it also naturally creates a circle that facilitates everyone being able to see and hear each other. Before I shared the conversation nugget, there was some commentary in the group of the need for a group like this one, where theatre people and creatives can gather and have these conversations.

I began by reading a quote from M. Shawn Copeland as printed in *Empty Church*: "Eucharistic solidarity orients us to the cross of the lynched Jesus of Nazareth, where we grasp the enormity of suffering, affliction, and oppression, as well as apprehend our complicity in the suffering, affliction, and oppression of others."[9] I honestly had to read it a couple times for them to absorb what was being discussed. I transitioned out of the quote by presenting the idea of our gathering around a meal (communion): Does our gathering orient us to the cross of the lynched Jesus?

The term "lynched" resonated with many as it was a catalyst to different thinking. One of our newer members then shared about a television show that she had watched recently that compared white and black men and their view of race, first interviewing them a couple decades ago and then following up with those same men today. I also highlighted a then-recent Facebook post by one of our members that discussed the theatre community's tendency to cast in ways that demean larger people. This became a robust conversation on body image, body positivity, and prior casting experiences.

I also note that the evening revealed a propensity within this demographic to talk about current productions that they are working on. I had noted in my journal that maybe curtailing people's talking about their current shows would diminish the possibility of bashing producers or directors. The conversation was germane to the topic, as it centered around the perceived complicity in oppression by us as actors, or those same producers and directors that were being maligned. It seemed to take a negative tone that should be avoided in the future, even given our freedom to express ourselves.

The last item of the evening was the riskiest: I asked if they wanted to continue meeting together. This was the moment that would determine if the past four gatherings merited continuation. It was unanimous to continue. I then asked about format: how many times would they like to gather, what they liked about what we had done thus far, and any other things that I had not considered.

9. Craigo-Snell, *Empty Church*, 108.

One member asked if we could bless the meal each time we gathered, especially considering the quote I shared this evening. His hope was that a blessing would help to orient us as we gathered. We agreed to meet once a month, sharing hosting responsibilities throughout the group. Potluck was determined to be the best manner of providing food for our time together. It was also determined that I would continue to mine for the nugget, at least for now.

I closed our time with a blessing: "Go in peace, create like crazy, and love one another." Thus, was completed the journey of launching this unique faith community.

Chapter 5

Dinner Theatre . . . Church?
Takes Flight

A YEAR IN THE LIFE OF DINNER THEATRE . . . CHURCH?

AFTER THREE MONTHS OF preliminary gatherings it was time to move into full-fledged *Dinner Theatre . . . Church?* gatherings. There were a few things that became apparent over the first few months of rolling these out: this type of gathering was needed and appreciated, people consistently attended and participated, and growth was possible moving forward. Therefore, beginning in September 2022 we officially launched *Dinner Theatre . . . Church?* (DTC)[1] as a consistent monthly gathering.

Over the course of a year we added new elements, we shared hosting responsibilities, and even began to encourage other people to mine for the nugget (develop the discussion topic) for each gathering. Each month featured a different topic as well as a different

---

1. Throughout most of this book I have referred to the new church gathering by its full title, *Dinner Theatre . . . Church?*, but in this journal retelling I have switched to DTC for ease of communication.

format, so the remainder of this chapter includes a synopsis of some of the gatherings (space does not allow for a complete recounting of all our times together), the nugget that was shared, and the positive or negative outcomes of each gathering time. I also include footnotes to what I read as inspiration for the nuggets, as these topics and elements might prove helpful to others seeking to develop groups like these in their own context.

September 2022

September marked the first gathering that was not hosted by me. The beauty of our gathering being hosted by another member is that it revealed ownership through hospitality and affirmed that it was not just my hosting that was drawing people, but that others saw fit to host and invite as well. We also added a new member who had been hoping to join but was not sure of the openness for new membership. After being assured that participation was open to anyone at any time, he happily joined in.

The nugget for our discussion came from Peter Heltzel's *Resurrection City*: "Transformation becomes a category that can deepen Boal's theater of the oppressed, as it is a call not only to the liberation of the oppressed, but also for the collective repentance of the oppressors."[2] This caused quite the lively discussion and oftentimes had to be reined in to focus on the intent of the nugget. One of the ways I was able to rein in the discussion was to ask those in attendance if we, as producers, are seeking to garner the repentance of oppressors—basically asking if we are using art manipulatively.

One member shared her husband's experience of the play *Seven*, produced by City on a Hill Arts, which deals with the lives of seven oppressed women and how they were able to rise above their circumstances to do amazing things. He mentioned that he felt poorly after seeing the play, because as a white male, he had no understanding of what it was like to be an oppressed woman. This

2. Heltzel, *Resurrection City*, 129.

actually confirmed Heltzel's point, because not only did that play lift up the oppressed women, it made room for a member of the oppressing class to wrestle with the content and how they may or may not be complicit in the oppression. Hopefully this can lead to repentance, which ultimately leads to liberation.

The fruit of the discussion included one more addition to our rules of life. We agreed that we needed to use "I talk" instead of generalities like "we" and "they"—and to take ownership of our complicity or experiences. We concluded by attempting to discern where we have been complicit in oppression in the past, which led to many expressing the hope that we continue the discussion next month.

October 2022

Once again, we gathered at another member's home and gathered around a bonfire in their backyard. I began our discussion by reading a few passages from *Theatrical Theology*, two of which I share here:

- "The Bible is not fundamentally a text. It was originally and should have always remained a drama: a drama with a script, for sure, but a drama that is rehearsed and improved anew in each setting, in each telling."[3]
- "Theatre should add a log to the fire of the revolution for radical social change."[4]

This set the stage for a reading from Matthew 23:23–28:

> Woe to you, scribes and Pharisees, hypocrites! For you tithe mint and dill and cumin, and have neglected the weightier matters of the law: justice and mercy and faithfulness. These you ought to have done, without neglecting the others. You blind guides, straining out a gnat and swallowing a camel! Woe to you, scribes and

3. Carter and Wells, "Holy Theatre," 227.
4. Heltzel, "Church as a Theatre of the Oppressed," 245.

Pharisees, hypocrites! For you clean the outside of the cup and the plate, but inside they are full of greed and self-indulgence. You blind Pharisee! First clean the inside of the cup and the plate, that the outside also may be clean. Woe to you, scribes and Pharisees, hypocrites! For you are like whitewashed tombs, which outwardly appear beautiful, but within are full of dead people's bones and all uncleanness. So you also outwardly appear righteous to others, but within you are full of hypocrisy and lawlessness.

What basically transpired after the readings was a time of confession as we continued the discussion from the month before. We delved into situations where we might have been complicit in oppression. Many difficult topics and experiences were shared. It was a wonderful time of honesty and transparency that I had yet to experience in a traditional church gathering. I was led to close in prayer because of the delicate nature of what had been shared. At that moment I felt that this gathering was truly a church in the biblical sense: community and accountability.

November 2022

November's gathering was entitled Friendsgiving as we have developed deep friendships over the past few months. We had a gathering of ten around my kitchen table. One of our members brought a grace to share from W. E. B. Dubois. These moments of grace, too, have become consistent elements of our gathering times and are often shared by someone other than me.

One of our readings for the evening came from *Noticing God*:

Culture is what we humans make of creation. Our cultural products give testimony to the reality of God when we have eyes to see and ears to hear. So it is that we turn in a God-ward direction under the power of a great symphony, through the transcendence of medieval murals in majestic European cathedrals, or via the mesmerizing vision of Dante's great poem, *Divine Comedy*. Our cultural products in all their creativity move us toward God.[5]

I then asked a chicken and egg question: as creatives, made in the image of God, do we create that which influences culture, or does culture dictate what we create?

The following is a statement from one of our members that was offered during discussions, which reveals the sacred in our midst:

> There is something profound that can happen when people try to deeply understand, or even empathize, with characters they disagree with, disapprove of, condemn. The act of imagining yourself as someone else, or what you would do if you were in someone else's situation, or held their beliefs, can be described as sacred, because it means recognizing that you are in the same community as [they are], the human race, the children of God as some would say. That is where compassion and true personal growth begins. And of course, artists, writers, actors, they create that act of imagination for others to experience, by doing it first for themselves.

This sentiment was offered from someone who identifies as an atheist yet is so profound in the way that it shares the heart of Christ—as one who became flesh, became one of us, in order to bring restored communion and shalom to the Earth. There is a powerful parallel between the theatre artist as one who embodies a character, and Christ, who took on flesh. It is so very important that we as Christ-followers learn empathy for the other in our midst, especially for those with whom we disagree.

February 2023

The synergy of City on a Hill Arts and DTC provides much fodder for our discussions. This time it was the more recent production

---

5. Peace, *Noticing God*, chap. 6.

of *An Act of God*, which is a comedy that presents God's new Ten Commandments. It is an irreverent piece that could easily offend those from a more conservative background. Regardless, it created much conversation, not only for us, but for the audience. As for DTC, we talked about the concept of God as an angry God.

In *An Act of God*, God refers to Godself as an "asshole" and uses the terms *racist* and *misogynist* in reference to Godself. This is what we unpacked that evening. Some questions that were considered were the following:

- Is there a connection between the Old Testament God and the New Testament God as revealed in Christ?

- Do we make God in our image or are we made in the image of God?

- Which image is correct?

I then shared the parable of the prodigal son (which one of our members had never heard prior to our gathering). The purpose of sharing this story was to flesh out what we can learn about God's heart for God's children. This evening's conversation was one of the more specifically Bible-based conversations, and yet, even though there were atheists and other non-Christians in our group, there was so much respect in the room.

April 2023

We continued to rotate hosting responsibilities and each person brought something to share for the meal. These shared foods remind me of Orthodox communion, where the gifts are brought to the altar to be shared and blessed. In this way, we were truly experiencing communion—we gave of ourselves to each other.

This gathering fell immediately after Easter, so I felt it timely to share a synopsis of the Easter story, ending with the concept that something had to die to provide new life. This was the nugget for the evening, inspiring conversation based on what had to die in our lives/art/world for something else to be reborn. I share some of the commentary here, as it was a deeply profound conversation.

- Unforgiveness has to die in order to give new life to a relationship.

- Pruning in our schedules needs to happen to release new life/ priority into passions.

- Controlling one's emotional personhood had to die so that new life would be revealed as being more connected to their true self.

- Bullshit had to die so that new life would be released into their interests.

- Fear had to die to bring new life into new adventures and new employment.

- Pride as a parent had to die to bring new life in their relationship with their son.

Transparency is paramount in this group and fosters trust and deeper relationships. The discussion on this evening made room for someone in the group to share an important change in their family: their child announced that they were transgender. This brought about a particular death-to-life statement in that they were mourning the loss of their son in a way, but rejoicing in the birth of their daughter. Language such as this, when referring to transgender people, can be hurtful, so it was especially powerful that the group allowed this individual to process what they had experienced on Easter Sunday. This was a beautiful evening that included the recognition of safe space, and that space made room for this person to share without negative commentary. Moments like these define the ethos of this group.

May 2023

This gathering marked the first time that someone other than me provided the nugget for the evening. This sharing of leadership was an important milestone for this group. It was especially profound as the leader chose to share a nugget that focused on forgiveness. They shared a reading based on the Apple TV show, *Ted Lasso*:

> How are we meant to react when really bad things happen to us? Sam Obisanya [Toheeb Jimoh] is angry when his beloved restaurant is broken into and ruined with doors, glass and furniture smashed. It's a horrible hate crime. Fortunately, his dad, Ola, [Nonso Anozie] is visiting from Nigeria, on hand to give him advice. "Anger will only weaken you and if you really want to piss off the people who did this, forgive them," he tells Sam.
>
> It's a tried and trusted trick encouraged by psychologists who argue that remaining angry with someone confines us to a state of victimhood. Until we forgive, we remain locked out of the possibility of healing. Remember Ted's philosophy about how we should be goldfish when insults come our way because goldfish have a ten-second memory and are therefore the happiest animals in the world?[6]

What transpired next was nothing short of wondrous and beautiful. One of our members shared intimately recent events in their life and how they were struggling with forgiving someone very close to them. There were tears coupled with gut-wrenching honesty. This community responded with grace, offering support and the beauty of silence as they listened and held space for their friend. What has been fostered in this faith family is space where the kingdom can break in—holy moments such as these where healing happens and the Spirit moves.

We concluded our time by sharing in a sacred act: we wrote down areas of our lives where we needed help with forgiveness and then placed them into the fire. As Vanhoozer writes, "The story cannot mean on its own; it becomes meaningful only when it is embodied in the concrete practices of the church."[7] These papers, these prayers, rose like incense heavenward. These moments were holy and confirmed the need for this community.

6. Broadbent, "How Ted Lasso Inspires," paras. 2–4.

7. Vanhoozer, *Drama of Doctrine*, 96.

June 2023

This was the last gathering before our one-year anniversary. It was hosted by one of our members, who also brought the nugget for the evening. What marked this gathering was my absence due to an emergency visit to the hospital upon my return from a missions trip. Yet, they continued to meet, and even shared later that this gathering was memorable to many. Although I was not there, I trusted the host to lead well and to help facilitate conversation in a manner that honored the ethos and fabric of our gathering. They did not fail, as one of the questions posed has continued to bear fruit in the lives of those that were gathered.

July 2023—Our One-Year Anniversary

Like other events that mark milestones, this gathering included times of celebration and remembrance. Many shared how they had felt welcome from the start, and that they appreciated the role of DTC in their journeys. Many brought spouses to attend that might not have been part of the gatherings in the past year. The table offering reflected our first gathering a year before: a potato bar.

I thought it would be important to continue the tradition of bringing a nugget to inspire our discussion. The first two came from *The Drama of Doctrine*:

- The church must be an agent of *shalom* working not simply for a cessation of hostilities but toward a restoration of friendly relations and, at the limit, of table fellowship.[8]
- The church participates fittingly in the theo-drama [here I explained that term as the overarching narrative of creation from beginning to end] when it becomes a theater of reconciliation, a display of divine and human forgiveness, a spectacle of God's love for the world.[9]

---

8. Vanhoozer, *Drama of Doctrine*, 435.
9. Vanhoozer, *Drama of Doctrine*, 362.

By using these definitions of church, I was able to encourage this gathering that they were truly a church—not a traditional one, but something new that was being born by the Spirit.

I concluded the evening by making one final ask of them: to consider being part of the podcast that I was hoping to create. The podcast would include their stories in hopes of encouraging others that, like them, needed community and a place to wrestle with spirituality and faith. I was blessed to receive affirmation by many that they would participate and share their stories.

DTC continues to meet monthly, sharing duties of hospitality as well as mining for the nugget. They have become a family and a church in the best possible way.

Summary and Conclusion

MY PURPOSE AND GOAL was to reach unchurched people that are part of the theatre community in North Central Massachusetts. The means to do so was developing a new church expression comprised of theatre artists, some of them members of the LGBTQ+ community, and implementing a means of constructing dialog in the *lingua franca* of the theatre for the purpose of discipleship in matters of faith.

In the Introduction and chapter 1 I was able to reveal that church trends in Massachusetts reveal a decline in church attendance, a decline in the belief in God, and a denial of the authority of Scripture. Church planting, as a solution to these trends, was discussed and presented, with the format of fresh expression churches creating a niche opportunity for a theatre community church.

I also highlighted the history of each step toward planting this church: my own personal history, my investment in the local theatre community, the planting of Sanctuary and the creation of City on a Hill. Relationship-building has been a key element in the implementation and success of this new church expression. Without having invested twenty years into the theatre community or having developed trust and respect with theatre people and LGBTQ+ individuals, I do not believe that this gathering would have been as impactful or long-lasting.

In chapters 2 and 3 I provided the theological groundwork for a theatre church and spiritual community that is affirming, loving, and healing. I drew the comparisons between theatre and church in areas of God's presence, embodied discipleship, and enacted justice. I also established the theological foundations for developing new expressions of church within, and for, the theatre community. Finally, in part two I attempted to provide ground-work that could bring Pentecostal theology and Queer theology closer in three areas: language and behavior, our treatment of LGBTQ+ youth, and hermeneutics. With these commitments in place, I believe it is possible to establish safe space to encounter the truth of the gospel for LGBTQ+ individuals.

In part three (chapters 4 and 5) I shared the journey of launching, and then continuing, this new church expression called *Dinner Theatre . . . Church?*

There are a few milestone markers that prove the success of this new faith family:

1. There is consistent attendance each month, with most people attending each month. For most of the community, theatre conflicts are the only things that keep them from attending (i.e.. rehearsals, tech weeks, etc.).

2. Hosting duties have been shared by all that have space in their homes to host our community. This was the first ele-ment that was shared amongst the members and continues to be an important part of ownership.

3. Mining of the discussion nugget has also been delegated to others. This is an important development as it takes the focus off me as the church planter and places it into the hands of the community itself. They have grown to desire input into what fuels our discussion.

4. My attendance is not necessary. This became abundantly evi-dent when I had to have emergency eye surgery. They con-tinued to meet without me. What is most interesting is that the evening I missed was one that was remembered fondly during the podcast interviews.

Podcast interviews after our one-year anniversary yielded the most affirming feedback. I asked each participant the same series of questions to get broad yet consistent data. I hesitate to use the formal term *data* because they were simply sharing their stories and their lives, but these stories affirm the need for and importance of *Dinner Theatre . . . Church?* The questions I asked were:

1. Who is [blank]? Basically, I asked them to tell me who they were: what they enjoy doing, what makes them tick.

2. What is your faith background, if any?

3. What is it about the invitation to *Dinner Theatre . . . Church?* that caused you to respond positively and attend?

4. What made you continue attending?

5. Was there an event or experience that was particularly meaningful to you during this past year?

6. Do you have any suggestions or encouragement to offer someone that might be interested in launching a church like this, or someone that is looking for community like this?

There were some consistencies in people's feedback as captured in the podcast recordings. First, they all shared the importance of having a safe place to share their thoughts, or even their struggles. This safe place was not happenstance, but was cultured and stipulated. This is due in part to the rules of life that we had established in the beginning. Many of the more memorable and meaningful experiences were born from the shared safe space that had been intentionally created.

Another resounding theme was the need for consistent community. Participating in theatre productions produces community. Johnson and Savidge confirm, "Humans are created to live in community; theater is an art form that naturally creates a community—an intimate and immediate community."[1] Although theatre can create community, that same essence of community slowly dissipates then disappears once a show closes. Very few

1. Johnson and Savidge, *Performing the Sacred*, 63.

people retain deep relationships post-show. The community that has been created through *Dinner Theatre . . . Church?* is deeper and more authentic than many had experienced before through theatre productions. I believe that it is the reason that our members continue to return month after month.

In addition, many of the podcast participants shared that the common affinity of theatre was a draw to being a part of this gathering. As one member said, "You like food, I like food." It seems simple, but the truth is that having a common bond, especially one as transformative as theatre, created the foundational element whereby deeper relationships and authentic conversations could be built. This shared affinity toward theatre can also be a distraction, as many participants will bring a conversation into the realm of complaining about prior experiences with local theatre groups. My goal is to try to avoid such discussions as they often will degrade into gossip, which negatively impacts the safe space that is needed to foster these discussions.

Finally, the most relevant feedback I heard was the importance of relationships. Their connection with me was critical to feeling comfortable to attend. For those that are seeking to begin a new church like this one, it is important to know that investment into people and their lives is critical. Sometimes that means decades of developing friendships and listening to people's stories.

The typical metrics used to gauge the success of a new church expression are not evident in this community yet and might never be evident. I have not baptized anyone, no one has made a declaration of accepting Jesus as their personal savior, nor has anyone chosen to tithe into the finances to support this gathering. Yet this gathering has fostered some of the most meaningful conversations I have experienced in more than twenty-five years of ministry. The ministry of Jesus is discussed and applied to our lives, and there is a beautiful ethos of support, love, and encouragement. So, in many ways it is a church. Only God knows what the future holds for this gathering, but for now we continue to meet monthly to encounter the Divine in our midst and that, in and of itself, is beautiful.

Appendix A

"Pull up a Chair" podcast can be found on the following platforms:

Spotify: https://open.spotify.com/show/1C534pHZtvE8hl6dCSRqoz.

Amazon: https://music.amazon.com/podcasts/016243f7-d635-40e6-a81c-cb24ea6f5694/pull-up-a-chair.

Apple Podcasts: https://podcasts.apple.com/us/podcast/pull-up-a-chair/id1711677559.

The first podcast was released October 16, 2023, with additional episodes being launched weekly on Mondays for a total of seven thematic episodes and one bonus episode.

Appendix B

THE FOLLOWING IS OFFERED as an example of how to engage with Scripture with an understanding of hermeneutic plurality. As mentioned earlier in this work, many authors have taken the time to write about specific verses that have been used to classify LGBTQ+ as sinful. In this appendix I will look at only one verse among those verses and show how there can be more than one way to faithfully read Scripture. I have chosen the verses from Romans 1 as my example text. I quote theologians and academics from a multitude of perspectives in order to reveal that there is more than one way to faithfully encounter the word of God.

The Scripture that is the focus of this appendix is from Romans 1:26–27:

> For this reason God gave them up to dishonorable passions. For their women exchanged natural relations for those that are contrary to nature; and the men likewise gave up natural relations with women and were consumed with passion for one another, men committing shameless acts with men and receiving in themselves the due penalty for their error.

I begin with a more conservative approach by quoting Douglas J. Moo in his commentary on the NIV version of Romans. He first asserts that "Some too quickly go with the flow and read the change in culture into the Bible, others so strongly resist the flow that they go beyond what the Bible says."[1] He continues:

---

1. Moo, *NIV Application Commentary*, 66.

Other interpreters have seized on the language of "against nature" that Paul uses in 1:26–27 to argue that those whom Paul condemns here are only those who practice homosexuality when it is against their own nature. In other words, it would be wrong for a person with a heterosexual orientation to engage in homosexual relations, but not for a person with a "natural" homosexual orientation. The problem with this view is a failure to understand Paul's "nature" language against its proper background. Paul is using this word as other Jewish writers did, to refer to the natural order of things as *ordained by God*.[2]

In addition, Moo affirms the view that homosexuality is sinful, albeit not any more sinful than any other sin.

> Nor is it so clear that the Bible presents homosexual activity as a perversion worse than any other—as many Christians have thought. To be sure, Romans 1 singles out homosexual activity for special attention. But Paul's purpose in doing so may not be because he regards it as a more serious sin than others but because he sees it as a particularly clear illustration of the violation of the created order. In any case, we are clearly called on to offer the same love and hope through the gospel to homosexuals that we offer to any caught up in any forms of sin.[3]

James Brownson, representing the mainline Protestant view, also addresses cultural context when reading Romans 1, but develops a different understanding than Moo. Here is Brownson, writing in *Bible, Gender, Sexuality: Reframing the Church's Debate on Same-Sex Relationships*:

> Another Roman writer, Dio Cassius, comments negatively on how Gaius was the only emperor to claim to be divine and to be the recipient of worship during his own lifetime. Gaius also tried at one point to erect a statue of himself in the Temple in Jerusalem; he was dissuaded only by a delegation from Herod Agrippa. Hence the link between Gaius and idolatry would have

2. Moo, *NIV Application Commentary*, 66.

3. Moo, *NIV Application Commentary*, 67.

been well-known indeed, particularly in Jewish circles. But Gaius also serves as "Exhibit A" for out-of-control lust. Suetonius reports how Gaius "lived in perpetual incest with all his sisters, and at a large banquet he placed each of them in turn below him, while his wife reclined above." He records gruesome examples of Gaius's arbitrary violence, vindictiveness, and cruelty. Later, Suetonius chronicles Gaius's sexual liaisons with the wives of dinner guests, raping them in an adjoining room and then returning to the banquet to comment on their performance. Various same-sex sexual encounters between Gaius and other men are similarly recounted. Finally, a military officer whom he had sexually humiliated joined a conspiracy to murder him, which they did less than four years into his reign. Suetonius records that Gaius was stabbed through the genitals when he was murdered. One wonders whether we can hear an echo of this gruesome story in Paul's comments in Romans 1:27: "Men committed shameless acts with men and received in their own person the due penalty for their error." Gaius Caligula graphically illustrates the reality of which Paul speaks in Romans 1: the movement from idolatry to insatiable lust to every form of depravity, and the violent murderous reprisal that such behavior engenders.[4]

Ethicist David P. Gushee continues Brownson's train of thought by explaining:

> If Paul had the imperial court in mind while painting his broad brushstrokes about the idolatrous debauchery of the Gentile word, that would mean that Romans 1:18–32 (look at that whole description again in this light) might have functioned as a highly evocative, deeply contextual, thickly veiled depiction of the Roman imperial court as a macabre worst-case symbol of Gentile depravity.[5]

My last theological resource is from Matthew Vine, who is well-known in Assemblies of God circles, even if people disagree with his theological take on this Scripture. There is much that he

---

4. Brownson, *Bible, Gender, Sexuality*, 157.
5. Gushee, *Changing Our Mind*, 88.

addresses regarding Romans 1, but here I will quote a short section that deals with the concepts of "natural" and "unnatural" considering the previous quote from Moo:

> In the ancient world, if a man took the active role in sex, his behavior generally was deemed to be "natural." But if he took the passive role, he was derided for engaging in "unnatural" sex. The opposite was true for women: sexual passivity was termed "natural," while sexual dominance was "unnatural."

Same-sex relations challenged those beliefs about nature and sex by putting a male in the passive role or a female in the active role. This inversion of accepted gender roles, combined with the non-procreative character of same-sex unions, is why ancient writers called same-sex behavior "unnatural."

> Plato, who lived and wrote more than four hundred years before Paul, is a leading example. In his dialogue *Laws*, Plato contrasted "natural" sex between men and women "for the purpose of procreation" with "unnatural" sex between same-sex partners. In another dialogue, Plato emphasized the problem of gender-role transgressions in same-sex unions. As Plutarch would later quote him, same-sex behavior is shameful because it involves "weakness and effeminacy on the part of those who, contrary to nature, allow themselves in Plato's words 'to be covered and mounted like cattle.'"[6]

Finally, I present a historical viewpoint, one that takes a deep dive into Roman culture to help us understand the context of the text. Sarah Ruden, who is not a theologian *per se*, but an anthropologist, writes:

> The active partner had no comeback from his callous and selfish behavior. There were no derogatory names for him. Except for some restraint to avoid conflict within his actual household, he positively strutted between his wife, his girlfriends, female slaves and prostitutes, and males. Penetration, after all, signaled moral uprightness—sorry

---

6. Vine, *God and the Gay Christian*, chap. 6.

about the image. We get our word "virtua" from the Latin *virtus*, literally "manliness"; courage, honesty, and responsibility were strongly linked to physical virility in the Greek and Roman minds.

In fact, society pressures a man into sexual brutality toward other males. To keep it unmistakable that he had no sympathy with passive homosexuals, he would tout his attacks on vulnerable young males. Encolpius (Crotcher), the narrator in Petronius, who dramatizes his loathing of the *cinaedus* [a man who did not conform to conventional Roman notions of masculinity] so memorably, is an unashamed and enthusiastic pederast (especially of a youngster that he shows in the role of Lucretia, a chaste, raped heroine of legend), though he chases women, too.[7]

Ruden then goes on to explain how we might envision Paul's reasoning behind his text in Romans:

In the Greco-Roman as well as the Jewish tradition, outrageous cruelty or exploitation insulted divinity, which was roused to avenge the helpless. The Greeks and Romans didn't have a thoroughly just god in their traditional pantheon to correct these balances in the universe; usually the Greek Zeus or the Roman Jupiter, as supreme ruler, would have to do. Sometimes the polytheists invoked an unnamed God, or a personification, Justice. Two or more deities might work together. But in any case, judgment was coming, and the arrogant and power-hungry were going to be sorry.[8]

I have presented here a small sampling of the variety of interpretations of Scripture, all being done with due diligence and research. When confronted with a hermeneutic plurality, we should agree that it is not possible to know the ultimate truth, and therefore, we should err on the side of grace.

Even Paul, earlier in his letter to the Roman church, states: "For I am not ashamed of the gospel, for it is the power of God for

---

7. Ruden, *Paul Among the People*, 53–54.

8. Ruden, *Paul Among the People*, 69–70.

salvation to everyone who believes, to the Jew first and also to the Greek. For in it the righteousness of God is revealed from faith for faith, as it is written, 'the righteous shall live by faith'" (Rom 1:16–17). This all-welcoming invitation is a gift of grace from a God who desires communion with God's creation. According to Moo, "Announcing what will become a key note in this letter, Paul insists that the salvation available in the gospel is for *all* who believe. In a significant advance on the Old Testament, which focused on Israel, the gospel is universally available."[9] He goes on to explain the concept of righteousness by writing, "What God does for us in justification is similar to what the judge does in a law court: He does not change the defendant by turning him or her into a new kind of person; rather, he declares the defendant innocent of the charges brought against him or her."[10]

This is the beauty and life-changing impact of extending grace. According to Paul J. Achtemeier:

> That is the incredible good news announced in the gospel. That is why the gospel must be brought to all people of every race and every cultural attainment. With God's act in Christ, all former boundaries have been removed, those that had existed between Jews and gentiles as well as those that had stood between sinful humanity and a righteous God. It is therefore no longer our task to remove boundaries or impediments. Our task is to accept the good news that those boundaries have been removed and that our way to a righteous and merciful God is no longer barred by the race into which we have been born or by what we may have done in the past.[11]

In Jesus' story about the wedding feast (Matt 22:1–14), he implores us to go to the highways and byways, bidding all to come to the table. Let us extend Jesus' table with grace and mercy.

---

9. Moo, *NIV Application Commentary*, 51.

10. Moo, *NIV Application Commentary*, 56.

11. Achtemeier, *Romans*, 37.

Bibliography

Achtemeier, Paul J. *Romans. Interpretation: A Bible Commentary for Teaching and Preaching*. Louisville: Westminster John Knox, 2010.

AG.org. "Assemblies of God Sixteen Fundamental Truths." https://ag.org/Beliefs/Statement-of-Fundamental-Truths.

———. "Homosexuality, Marriage, and Sexual Identity." https://ag.org/Beliefs/Position-Papers/Homosexuality-Marriage-and-Sexual-Identity.

Boal, Augusto. *Theatre of the Oppressed*. New York: Theatre Communications Group, 1985.

Bolz-Weber, Nadia. *Pastrix: The Cranky, Beautiful Faith of a Sinner & Saint*. New York: Jericho, 2013.

Broadbent, Lucy. "How Ted Lasso Inspires Us to Fight Forward, Not Back." *Women Love Tech*, May 25, 2023. https://womenlovetech.com/how-ted-lasso-inspires-us-to-fight-forward-not-back/.

Brook, Peter. *The Empty Space*. New York: Scribner, 1968.

Brownson, James V. *Bible, Gender, Sexuality: Reframing the Church's Debate on Same-Sex Relationships*. Grand Rapids: Eerdmans, 2013.

Callaway, Kutter, and Dean Batali. *Watching TV Religiously: Television and Theology in Dialogue*. Grand Rapids: Baker Academic, 2016.

Carter, Richard, and Samuel Wells. "Holy Theatre: Enfleshing the Word." In *Theatrical Theology*, edited by Wesley Vander Lugt and Trevor Hart, 224–40. Eugene, OR: Cascade, 2014.

Cheng, Patrick S. *From Sin to Amazing Grace: Discovering the Queer Christ*. New York: Seabury, 2012.

———. *Radical Love: Introduction to Queer Theology*. Kindle ed. New York: Seabury, 2011.

Craigo-Snell, Shannon. *The Empty Church: Theater, Theology, and Bodily Hope*. Oxford: Oxford University Press, 2014.

Dearborn, Kerry. *Drinking from the Wells of New Creation: The Holy Spirit and the Imagination in Reconciliation*. Eugene, OR: Cascade, 2014.

Durst, D. L. "The Nations." In *The Lexham Bible Dictionary*, edited by John D. Barry, Logos Software. Bellingham, WA: Lexham, 2016.

Fujimura, Makoto. *Culture Care: Reconnecting with Beauty for Our Common Life*. Downers Grove, IL: InterVarsity, 2017.

Gabbatt, Adam. "Losing Their Religion: Why US Churches Are on the Decline." *The Guardian*, January 22, 2023. https://www.theguardian.com/us-news/2023/jan/22/us-churches-closing-religion-covid-christianity.

Glassgold, Judith M., and Caitlyn Ryan. "The Role of Families in Efforts to Change, Support, and Affirm Sexual Orientation, Gender Identity, and Expression in Children and Youth." In *The Case Against Conversion "Therapy": Evidence, Ethics, and Alternatives*, edited by Douglas D. Haldeman, 89–107. Washington, DC: American Psychological Association, 2022.

Gushee, David P. *Changing Our Mind*. Canton, MI: Read the Spirit, 2017.

Hays, Christopher B., and Richard B. Hays. *The Widening of God's Mercy: Sexuality Within the Biblical Story*. New Haven, CT: Yale University Press, 2024.

Hays, Richard B. *The Moral Vision of the New Testament: A Contemporary Introduction to New Testament Ethics*. San Francisco: Harper Collins, 1996.

Heltzel, Peter. "The Church as a Theatre of the Oppressed: The Promise of Transformational Theater for a Youth-Led Urban Revolution." In *Theatrical Theology*, edited by Wesley Vander Lugt and Trevor Hart, 241–62. Eugene, OR: Cascade, 2014.

———. *Resurrection City: A Theology of Improvisation*. Grand Rapids: Eerdmans, 2012.

Horton, Stanley M. *What the Bible Says About the Holy Spirit*. Springfield, MO: Gospel House, 2005.

John, Elton. "Interview." *Music Monthly Magazine*, a supplement to *The Observer*, 2006.

Johnson, Todd E., and Dale Savidge. *Performing the Sacred: Theology and Theatre in Dialogue*. Grand Rapids: Baker Academic, 2009.

Johnston, Robert K. *God's Wider Presence: Reconsidering General Revelation*. Grand Rapids: Baker Academic, 2014.

Johnston, Robert K., Craig Detweiler and Kutter Callaway. *Deep Focus: Film and Theology in Dialogue*. Grand Rapids: Baker Academic, 2019.

Kim, Grace Ji-Sun, and Graham Hill. *Healing Our Broken Humanity: Practices for Revitalizing the Church and Renewing the World*. Downers Grove, IL: InterVarsity, 2018.

Malphurs, Aubrey. *The Nuts and Bolts of Church Planting: A Guide for Starting Any Kind of Church*. Grand Rapids: Baker, 2011.

Manneh, Elizabeth. "Lectio Divina: A Beginner's Guide." March 1, 2023. https://bustedhalo.com/ministry-resources/lectio-divina-beginners-guide.

Marin, Andrew. *Love Is an Orientation: Elevating the Conversation with the Gay Community*. Downers Grove, IL: InterVarsity, 2009.

McNamara, Mary. "Night's Best and Worst Moments." *Los Angeles Times*, September 18, 2025.

Moltmann, Jurgen. *The Church in the Power of the Spirit*. Minneapolis: Fortress, 1993.

Moo, Douglas M. *The NIV Application Commentary: Romans*. Grand Rapids: Zondervan, 2000.

Peace, Richard. *Noticing God*. Kindle ed. Downers Grove, IL: InterVarsity, 2012.

Pew Research Center. "Religious Landscape Study: Adults in Massachusetts." https://www.pewresearch.org/religion/religious-landscape-study/state/massachusetts.

Pike, Steve. *Next Wave: Discovering the 21st Century Church*. Kindle ed. St. Charles, MO: ArtSpeak Creative, 2022.

Ruden, Sarah. *Paul Among the People: The Apostle Reinterpreted and Reimagined in His Own Time*. New York: Image, 2010.

Shelton, Ron, dir. *Bull Durham*. Los Angeles: Orion Pictures, 1988.

The Trevor Project. "2022 National Survey on LGBTQ Youth Mental Health." https://www.thetrevorproject.org/survey-2022/#suicide-by-sexual-orientation.

Van Der Leeuw, Gerardus. *Sacred and Profane Beauty: The Holy in Art*. Oxford: Oxford University Press, 2006.

Vander Lugt, Wesley. *Living Theodrama: Reimagining Theological Ethics*. Surrey, UK: Ashgate, 2014.

Vanhoozer, Kevin J. *The Drama of Doctrine: A Canonical Linguistic Approach to Christian Theology*. Louisville: Westminster John Knox, 2005.

Vine, Matthew. *God and the Gay Christian: The Biblical Case in Support of Same-Sex Relationships*. Kindle ed. Colorado Springs: Convergent, 2014.

Wagner, C. Peter. *Church Planting for a Greater Harvest: A Comprehensive Guide*. Eugene, OR: Wipf and Stock, 1990.

Yang, Daniel. "Four Trends Shaping Church Planting and Growth Through 2050." March 30, 2021. https://research.lifeway.com/2021/03/30/4-trends-shaping-church-planting-and-growth-through-2050/.

Index

Page numbers followed by "n" and another number refer to a footnote on that page.